An
ETERNITY
of EAGLES

An ETERNITY of EAGLES

THE HUMAN HISTORY OF THE MOST FASCINATING BIRD IN THE WORLD

STEPHEN J. BODIO

Lyons Press
Guilford, Connecticut
An Imprint of Globe Pequot Press

Lyons Press is an imprint of Globe Pequot Press.

Project editor: Heather Santiago
Layout: Maggie Peterson
Text design: Maggie Peterson

Library of Congress Cataloging-in-Publication Data is available on file.

ISBN 978-0-7627-8022-8

Printed in the United States of America

10 9 8 7 6 5 4 3 2 1

TABLE OF CONTENTS

To the late Aralbai of Bayaan Olgii and the very much alive Lauren McGough of Oklahoma, Mongolia, Scotland, and who knows where next: Berkutchis.

INTRODUCTION

By Annie Proulx

Some decades ago I, with several other people, was involved with a natural history writing program in Vermont, all of us trying to guide makers of mud ball prose in their journey toward clarity and grace. Several of the instructors had rooms in the same building and shared a common kitchen. At the end of the second day, I looked forward to a cold drink on the porch while watching evening bats in the twilight. I reached into the refrigerator's grim little ice cube compartment and pulled out a tray. Instead of ice cubes the cavities contained an assortment of moths, large and small. One was a luna moth, a creature I had not seen since I was a child. Had they made their way into the compartment during the weeks the refrigerator stood empty and gaping? But then the kitchen door opened and a tousle-headed man with glowing eyes came in.

"My moths!" he said to the ice cube tray, as one would say "my long-lost twin brother!" It was my first meeting with Steve Bodio, whom I knew only from his essays in *Gray's Sporting Journal*. I got used to seeing him crouched by the screen door at night waiting for new moth victims and to listening to monologues about startle patterns, mimicry, and melanism. Before the session was over, I knew this ardent biologist-naturalist a little better—a man who collected insects, raised pigeons, and hunted with falcons and hawks; collected rare books on the natural world; was vastly well read in history, paleontology, archaeology, and climatology; knew about ancient horses, the history and habits of the dog, and Egyptian mummification processes; could quote from Buffon, Charles Wilkes, William Bartram, Wilfred Thesiger, and the authors of little-known treatises on gyrfalcons and eagles;

an eager talker on all subjects. Years after I met him he contracted malaria in Zimbabwe and of course developed " . . . a fascination with parasite evolution." He was the kind of restlessly curious fellow who might have ended up living with some remote tribe. In fact he continued his examination of the world from a home base in one of the emptier regions of New Mexico in a house full of books, bones, dogs, and raptors and with a shady backyard mellifluous with his extensive pigeon collection. Eventually I lost touch with Bodio, for years depending on news from our mutual friends, Louise and Bob Jones, who always had a first-rate "Bodio story."

Bodio learned something of grief when his wife Betsy died. "No worst, there is none. Pitched past pitch of grief . . . "[1] His beautiful memorial book, *Querencia* (a reference to the "safe" place in the bull ring where the beleaguered bull takes his stand), was only briefly available before his amateur then-publisher decided bookstores were part of a corrupt system and locked the copies away. Only through the help of Montana writer friends and lawyers was he able to regain the copies and copyright. For several years after Betsy's death he stumbled around with various women until he met the extraordinary Elizabeth Adam (Libby)—archaeologist, Outward Bound guide, chef and caterer, mountain climber, world traveler, musician.

Bodio's passionate enthusiasm for animals and birds and his low interest in careerism have led him occasionally into shoal waters, and he has eked out a fingernail kind of living. He is a natural history writer with an unquenchable desire to learn about the creatures that share the planet with humans. Following his interests has come at the cost of a decent income, partly because he is interested in such nonmainstream subjects as animal behavior and hunting, cockfights, falconry, and other blood sports in a time when people are increasingly estranged from the natural world and the harsh lives of nonhuman creatures in it; if it isn't domesticated, it doesn't count. As Bodio somewhat bitterly

---

1   Gerard Manley Hopkins. "No Worst ...," *Poems*, 1918.

puts it, " . . . I am, at least in today's journalistic niche ecosystem, classifiable as a 'travel writer' and a 'nature writer.'" His interests have taken him all over the world, in particular to Central Asia to be in the company of high-altitude falconers and eaglers.

Most birders are concerned primarily with making lists of the number of birds they have identified, a rather artificial category of knowledge that tells us little about ecosystems and specific habitats. I was surprised last year reading Jonathan Franzen's *The Discomfort Zone*. All Franzen's heart-wound writing urges one to reexamine oneself in the matrix of family and impinging crises. I was attracted to the section on his bird-watching period ("My Bird Problem"), enlivened with brilliant descriptions of several birds and his identification with birds, his journey from clumsy curiosity to headlong obsession. The birds metamorphosed into piteous, poor creatures; then somehow they became Franzen himself then became his mother, who was dying of colon cancer. In the end Franzen revealed himself as a species-list striver going for four hundred, and when he achieved that goal he became " . . . weary of birds and birding."[2]

Those of us who are interested in bird behavior beyond the feeder or the identification guidebook find meager pickings when it comes to information. I am fortunate that my house faces a cliff with a river at the base where I can watch raptors, waterfowl, and a hundred other species. The nests of a pair of bald eagles and another upriver inhabited by golden eagles are in sight from the breakfast table. I have plenty of books on birds, but the information on why the big eagles do what they do is hard to dig out. Eagle behavior is usually lumped together with the general behavior of the accipiters, but a single book that focused on the rich lore and sweep of eagledom did not seem to exist. For years I have relied on observation, folklore, and the eagle stories of a few rural neighbors and friends who take notice of them. Bodio's beautifully written and authoritative book *Eagles* is a primary

---

2   Jonathan Franzen. *The Discomfort Zone: A Personal History*. London: Fourth Estate, 2006, p. 195.

source of information as well as an omnium gatherum from literature, film, and mythology concerning these large, striking birds.

Birders are often puzzled by avian plumage that is not constant but changes with age, season, and locality. Keeping track of such variables for many species, plus pre-molt and molt stages, is terrifically complex. In an effort to simplify the birder's eternal question, "What bird is that?" the reductionist approach of bird identification guidebooks gives the impression of immutable species in a fixed world. Bodio, in his discussion of ever-branching cladistic analyses of changing species in transitional habitats, reminds us that species classifications are human constructs and that mutability is the common denominator of life. Once we grasp an idea of the fluid currents of changing habitats and climates and the creatures that fit themselves to those changes, we can look for adaptive and opportunistic behavior as well as size and feather color. This sense of modification underpins Bodio's book as he introduces us to the current eagle groups: the sea eagles, which include the familiar bald eagle; the snake eagles; jungle eagles; "odd" eagles; and booted eagles, considered the true eagles by most of us. The booted golden eagle, says Bodio, " . . . is the quintessential capital-E eagle, the Platonic ideal of a bird of prey . . . " Bodio also introduces us to unfamiliar eagles as the huge "flying wing" bateleurs of the sub-Sahara, the Indian black eagle with "paddle shaped" wings and exceedingly long tail, and the tiny little eagle of Australia.

His vivid description of an eagle, if it could imagine itself, is of a "carnivorous Buddhist." Through Bodio's insights we get a strange glimpse of these other minds that share the earth with us: "I believe that animals—birds and mammals anyway—do think, but they think in ways that might seem alien and frightening to us if we could inhabit their minds." We cannot inhabit their minds, but we can appreciate the gulf of distance between our two species, brilliantly illustrated here.

Humans are creatures who make categories. They range from "behaviors" like natural history, lives and loves, skills and powers, and parenting and nest-building; to "place," such as habitat and migration routes. There is a broad-ranging review of the eagle in human mythologies and ceremonies from Tibet to the pueblos of the American Southwest, in symbolism and art, in the journals of early travelers, and even in adventure novels and films constructed around the supposed fierce and noble characters of eagles. Notable is the film documentary *Kyran over Mongolia*, " . . . a brilliant and unflinching record of all of eagle training, from trapping the bird to her taking her first fox."

Bodio is himself a falconer and the chapter on eagle falconry (eaglry?) is particularly gripping: a history of the sport from the time of Marco Polo to modern-day Kazakhstan, where hunting wolves with trained female eagles is still important. The tradition of eagles as hunting partners persists to this day in central Asia. Bodio gives us an arresting contemporary image of the hunter riding out to the field on a motorcycle with his eagle in the sidecar. Where else can one learn of the unusual practices of Japanese falconers with the *kumataka*, or mountain hawk eagle, which their owners keep in a hawk house forbidden to children and pets for their safety?

Do eagles attack humans? Some cite the skull of the Taung Baby, an early hominid, which was found in association with a fossil bone midden of small animals very like the accumulation around a raptor nest site; they believe that two holes in the skull may have been made by an eagle—the huge crowned hawk eagle is implicated. Bodio discusses several authenticated examples of eagle damage to humans, from children to Aeschylus who, legend has it, died when an eagle dropped a tortoise on his head, apparently mistaking his bald pate for a stone. In our own near past, eagles were poisoned, snared, and hunted from the ground and from helicopters and planes by ranchers who believed the birds carried off young stock. Today the major group taking eagles alive or shooting them are American Indians, particularly the Hopi and Navajo. At a big powwow featuring ceremonial dancing, the remains of thousands of eagles stir the air at ground level. In recent years the eagle permit system for Indians and the associated eagle feather trade has stirred up considerable controversy.

And so now we have a fine eagle book to sit on the shelf with the bird guides, as Shelley wrote of Coleridge, "A hooded eagle among blinking owls."[3] May all interested in the wild world read it with enjoyment and enlightenment.

—Annie Proulx

Annie Proulx is the author of *The Shipping News* and three other novels, *That Old Ace in the Hole, Postcards,* and *Accordion Crimes;* the story collections *Heart Songs, Close Range, Bad Dirt,* and *Fine Just the Way It Is;* and *Bird Cloud: A Memoir of Place.* Her story "Brokeback Mountain," which originally appeared in the *New Yorker,* was made into an Academy Award–winning film. She has won the Pulitzer Prize, a National Book Award, the *Irish Times* International Fiction Prize, and the Pen/Faulkner Award, and is a fellow of the American Academy of Arts and Letters. She lives in Wyoming.

---

3   Percy Bysshe Shelley. "*Letter to Maria Gisborne,*" 1820.

PROLOGUE

"The way of the eagle in the air ... "

—PROVERBS 30:19

On a steeply slanting talus slope ten miles north of the little New Mexico town where I have lived for more than thirty years, a shadow falls across me, as silent and swift as a blowing cloud.

I should be ready. I know there is an eagle's nest tucked into a hollow in the vertical wall above. But the shadow crosses me as it must cross a prey animal, and I involuntarily flinch and stumble. The eagle, the great female, has materialized from the air like a spirit, a black hole in the sky. She stands on the wind less than a hundred feet away, surveys me with a cool gaze, then catches the wind with her fingered wings and blows down its stream.

The eagle's shadow has fallen on us since long before we were human. The Taung Baby, a 2.5-million-year-old skull of a prehuman South African *Australopithecine*, shows punctures[4] that anthropologists Lee Berger and Ron Clarke attributed to an eagle, perhaps one similar to *Stephanoaetus coronatus,* the modern African crowned eagle, still reliably implicated in attacks on children.[5] Eagles were big enough to be competitors, bold and intelligent enough to live near us without great danger, and beautiful, even magical, in their movement. Every culture that encountered them has left a written or pictorial account, from the ancient Greeks to the Japanese to the Aztecs, who knew the enormous crested harpy, whose name comes to us from the Greek for "snatcher." The Japanese in Hokkaido trained *Spizaetus nipalensis,* the mountain hawk eagle, calling it *kumataka,* "bear hawk";[6] it is strong enough to

---

4   Rick Gore. "The First Steps," *National Geographic,* vol. II (1997) p. 75.
5   Peter Steyn. *Birds of Prey of Southern Africa* (Dover, NH, 1983).
6   E. W. Jameson. *The Hawking of Japan* (Davis, CA, 1976) p.11.

A Golden eagle launches from its perch in this portrait by Russian artist Vadim Gorbatov. VADIM GORBATOV

kill foxes and small deer. Just before the arrival of Europeans, the Maoris of New Zealand may have been preyed upon by the largest eagle of all, which could kill ten-foot-tall moas. They left paintings of this fearsome predator on rock faces.[7]

The eagle known by most old societies is the one that lives on my mountain: the golden eagle; "the" eagle, *aetus Aquila* of the Romans; the "damn black Mexican eagle" of border sheepmen. Golden eagles are among the three or four largest predatory birds in the world and perhaps the most biologically successful. They live clear across North America, from Labrador to Mexico, in Siberia and all across Asia north of the Himalayas, and through the Middle East and Europe, down into the mountains of Morocco. Close relatives like the black, or Verreaux's, eagle and the wedge-tailed eagle inhabit South Africa

This sliding door panel is decorated with an imperial eagle, plum tree, and camellia. It's from seventeenth-century Japan, and was created during the Momoyama period. WIKICOMMONS

and Australia. Aquilas are the birds of prey with the closest relations to humans—antagonistic, appreciative, utilitarian, mythical, real, and theological—for uncounted thousands of years. They are actors in

---

7   Trevor Worthy & Richard Holdaway. *The Lost World of the Moa* (Indiana, 2002), p. 333.

Pueblo Indian rituals; their tail feathers are sacred to the Plains tribes. The ancient Romans, who gave the name *Aquila* to the species and later to the genus, used them as battle standards and war animals to attack the heads of their enemies. They were allegedly reserved for emperors in European falconry and are still used to hunt wolves in Central Asia and deer in Eastern Europe. They have been poisoned by Scottish sheepherders, accused of stealing babies, and hunted from single-engine airplanes in Texas as recently as the 1960s. Despite the assertions of some of their more sentimental defenders, goldens are

A golden eagle attacks a saiga antelope in Siberia in this nineteenth-century engraving. THE LIVING WORLD, ILLUSTRATED BY J. W. BUELL (PHILADELPHIA, PA, 1889)

capable of taking antelope and deer in the wild and, at least once, have been proven to kill calves.

Eagles are old—old in a way that humans, evolutionary infants, can barely comprehend. Aquila has seen human civilizations, Yeats's "old civilizations put to the sword," come and go and probably feasted on the remains, for eagles are not too proud to feast on others' meat. We don't know exactly how long the genus has been around, but many modern bird families were already flying during the late Cretaceous, time of the tyrannosaur and triceratops.

German artist Emil Doepler (1855–1922) painted this oil-on-canvas portrayal of an eagle and waterfall. WIKICOMMONS

Given the rarity of bird fossils (hollow bones are fragile to the point of evanescence to start with, and true eagles have always been inhabitants of the windy uplands rather than the sediment-rich basins that produce shales and fossils), it is likely that true eagles, identical to those alive today, were around to watch as our ancestors began

"Bearcootes" dramatically make war on wolves in this illustration.
Travels in the Regions of the Upper and Lower Amoor by Thomas Witlam Atkinson

to stand upright. Their shadows doubtless fell over the wandering bands of primates that exploded out of Africa less than a million years ago, long before those restless hominids began to build cities and civilizations. Aquila was always overhead, feasting on their leavings, nesting on cliffs over their first river-valley fields.

Because of the way they view the world, we do not "bother" eagles, though they always need what ecologists call a healthy prey base. A village and farm economy supports eagles very well. My ancestors in the Italian Alps doubtless knew the golden eagle; Aquila still lives in those places today. Years ago when I spent a month hiking around some obscure corners of northern Provence, I didn't expect to see eagles. The French are notorious for killing raptors; a nation of food-loving hunters with all the old-fashioned prejudices against predators, they only recently discovered that birds of prey are virtually irrelevant to gamebird populations. But to my surprise predatory birds considered rare in "greener" parts of Europe were everywhere. Red kites soared over a Roman coliseum that was still used for concerts; Bonelli's eagles, close relative of the noble Japanese *kumataka*, wheeled in courtship flights over oak copses beneath the bare teeth of the Dentelles de Montmirail. Best, one pair of eagles would come to us. In the early evening, as we ate our dinner in the courtyard of the presbytery in Serignan, two great snake-eating short-toed eagles, circaètes de Jean-le-Blanc, would soar over the village, drifting in high above the wheeling, screeching flocks of swifts that swirled around town like rush-hour traffic, and turn around and around in stately majesty, flashing snowy undersides as they banked in the setting sun.

The eagle's tolerance is not without limits. A real modern city of tens of thousands and more paves over their food supply. I grew up in Boston, so didn't live with eagles until I moved to rural New Mexico. Now if I wish to, I can see an eagle every day.

Legendary eagles of sorts live here too. Socorro County is where the only case of calf predation by eagles accepted by the Audubon Society took place, but those who understand eagles understand that "kill" does not mean "carry." Even a big golden has a hard time getting aloft with a large jackrabbit. Yet I spent one night drinking whiskey and trying to escape from the descendant of a rancher (he was not a rancher himself, which is probably significant) who insisted on telling me that he had seen two eagles fly off with a four-hundred-pound steer the previous winter. That this would be the equivalent of his carrying away an eighteen-wheeler cattle truck did not seem a diplomatic thing to say under the circumstances.

Eagles are not "like" us. The sentimental belief that an animal with which we identify is like us—or worse, *likes* us—is not the

As depicted in this fountain in Bratislava, Slovakia, Zeus, having taken the form of an eagle, transports Ganymede to Mount Olympus. Lukas Pobuda/Shutterstock.com

least of humans' common cultural mistakes. It's probably easier to "understand"—all these questions and approximations must be put in quotes once you think hard about them—an insect than an eagle! A bug's senses and drives may be utterly alien, but its behaviors are reflexive and mechanical in comparison to a warm-blooded vertebrate's. Eagles think and learn.

Our imagination fails to comprehend other animals. On one hand, Westerners often dismiss animals as a mass of insentient beings that merely respond to stimuli and do not think—Cartesian automatons. On the other, almost all cultures clothe human minds in different costumes, in feathers and fur and scales—better but still inadequate. We need new ways of imagining the minds of the "other bloods" (an excellent C. S. Lewis phrase) with which we share our world. Eagles contain power and intelligence in a body that weighs only twelve pounds. They appear and disappear like magic in seconds and can fall out of the sky to kill a one-hundred-pound antelope or a five-pound flying goose with no tools but the muscles of a hollow-boned body smaller than a child's. Those talons exert a ton of pressure at their tips. Aquila's enormous brown eyes, capable of resolving a hare's twitching ear at two miles, weigh more than its intelligent brain does.

Humans order experiences into stories, but nature has no plots, no ambitions, no internal conflicts; its endings are neither happy nor sad, because its other actors do not tell themselves stories the way we do. An eagle's perception of its own life might be of a bright eternal present like a carnivorous Buddhist's: confident, centered, and watchful, with a dim past and no thoughts or worries about the future. Perhaps it would be a bit like the protagonist's thoughts in Ted Hughes's poem "Hawk Roosting": "I hold creation in my foot / Or fly up, and revolve it all slowly— / I kill where I please because it's all mine / . . . Nothing has changed since I began."

Too many writers who write about animals either pretend to a scientist's assumed "objectivity," using the passive voice and a deliberate flattening of affect to distance themselves from the subject on the page, or else anthropomorphize their protagonists. I believe that animals *do* think but that they think in ways that might seem alien or even frightening to us if we could inhabit their minds. I said that eagles have no story, but they do. It's just that their story is so different from ours that a narration of it would make no "sense." What are we to make of a creature that, if well fed, will sit from dawn to dusk just watching? Or for whom it is moral, even right, to kill and eat its weaker sibling in the nest? Nobody but another eagle could experience a lifelike narrative of an eagle's life without spasms of boredom or horror.

These days predators are seen as utterly benign creatures in the popular imagination. Think of *The Lion King*, where prey animals appear as counselors to the hero. What do they think the lions eat? In such an atmosphere it's hard to resist quoting the old Canadian trapper who caught wolves for the Yellowstone restoration project. He allegedly said, "Ranchers think that wolves live on cows; environmentalists think they live on mice. They're both full of shit."

New England naturalist Henry Beston said it well in his book, *The Outermost House*:

> We need another and a wiser and perhaps a more mystical concept of animals. Remote from universal nature, and living by complicated artifice, man in civilization surveys the creature through the glass of his knowledge and sees thereby a feather magnified and the whole image in distortion. We patronize them for their incompleteness, for their tragic fate of having taken form so far below ourselves. And therein we err, and greatly err. For the animal shall not be measured by man. In a world older and more complete than ours they move finished and complete, gifted with extensions of the senses we have lost or never attained, living by voices we shall never hear.

They are not brethren, they are not underlings; they
are other nations, caught with ourselves in the net
of life and time, fellow prisoners of the splendor and
travail of the earth.

I am human, and wish I could fly with eagles and, liberated to the
air, hunt with them like a human mate—blowing down the wind like a
thought, a shadow on furled wings, falling from the sky like a sentient
thunderbolt to kill with my own suddenly powerful hands. The wish
to understand, to know, and even for a moment to be something
different, something other than human, is an entirely human desire;
an eagle would neither comprehend nor care. Our dreaming species
exists within a larger context that predates us; it is one that needs us
less than we need it.

CHAPTER 1

NATURAL HISTORY

" . . . endless forms most beautiful and most wonderful have been, and are being, evolved."
—CHARLES DARWIN

What is an eagle?

The *Oxford English Dictionary* says simply: "Any of the larger birds of prey which are not vultures" then goes on to describe the two species, the golden and white-tailed sea eagles, that are native to Britain. The *Oxford Dictionary of Natural History* refers to three categories: aquila, sea, and hawk eagles.

These definitions are neither adequate nor complete; by them, any large buteo hawk like the common buzzard or American red-tailed hawk, or large accipiter like the goshawk, would be an "eagle." In some instances the line blurs. The description of a Chinese "eagle" in Mark Elvin's *The Retreat of the Elephants* ("Their plumage is gray and black in an alternating pattern. Their bodies are as large as that of a goose. Their eyes are yellow and red; and the beak is sharply tapered and hooked"[8]) is plainly that of a goshawk.

But the word "eagle" in English refers almost arbitrarily to a number of different evolutionary lineages. They range in weight from one pound (454 grams) to over sixteen pounds (7 kilograms), perhaps as much as twenty; and in wingspan from only three feet (0.92 meter) to more than eight (2.4–plus meters). Various eagles eat snakes, fish, carrion, other birds, monkeys, deer, and the contents of birds' nests. They live from the arctic to the equator, in tundra, rain forest, mountain, and desert.

Not all eagles are closely related. The problem of classification— of which animal or plant is related to which—has occupied Western philosophers at least since the time of Aristotle. Until Charles Darwin's time, various similarities could be described, but did these actually represent relatives? If all life had been created separately, similarities were finally inexplicable. When Darwin's theory described how we all descend from a common ancestor, and are all ultimately related, the term "relative" began to make more than just metaphorical sense.

The modern version of the Darwinian system makes use of cladistics, a system that uses branching diagrams known as cladograms, or "trees," to illustrate relationships rather than showing evolution as an ever-rising line or predestined arrow. In the branching diagrams used to portray these relationships, the splitting of an evolutionary lineage always creates two equal "sister" groups, which in turn may split again—indefinitely.

Cladistic analysis of the relationships between organisms is in a constant state of flux as new information from genetic analysis, fossils, and other sources comes in. Right now snake "eagles" appear to branch off early in time, but so defined they include the huge Philippine, or monkey-eating eagle, whose size and habits would group it with the

---

8   Mark Elvin. *The Retreat of the Elephants* (New Haven, CT, and London, 2004), p. 308.

huge predatory harpy types. These harpy eagles, and booted eagles—the group feathered to the toes that includes Aquila—branch off later, separately, as do sea eagles and their relatives.[9]

These relationships, though tentatively valid (*all* scientific conclusions are tentatively valid; as Australian zoologist Tim Flannery says, "sooner or later all scientific hypotheses will be proven wrong or irrelevant"[10]) do not always group well with intuitive, apparent, or folk taxonomies. In the book by Martin Wallen he writes of the fox and its many forms:

> Henry's account of fox ambiguity helps to make
> sense of how 21 widely different animals could
> come to be identified as "fox." If modern taxonomy
> recognizes the fox as an animal that can take 21
> different forms, can exist in almost any habitat and
> manifests extremely different dispositions, then it
> has entirely overturned the Aristotelian need for
> distinct unchanging characteristics. But the fox
> also causes problems for modern scientists who do
> not embrace its ambiguity as easily as Henry does,
> for since the nineteenth century naturalists have
> established, de-classified, and re-classified numerous
> canid species as foxes, expanding the genera of "fox"
> to accommodate the divergences found among all the
> foxes of the world.[11]

I am not sure that modern scientists fear ambiguity with some existential unease; their efforts to redefine relationships are the product of an ever-richer information environment. But to understand what

---

9 Darrin Naish. Personal communication.
10 Tim Flannery. *Chasing Kangaroos* (New York, 2004), p. 118.
11 Martin Wallen. *Fox* (London, 2006), p. 25.

kinds of eagles exist, we can now leave behind the constant revisions of taxonomy and look at the different niches, habits, and appearances of the birds we call "eagle."

By my count there are (currently—remember, all these are subject to revision!) sixty-nine species officially called "eagle" in English.[12] These include thirty booted eagles, twenty-one snake eagles, ten fish eagles, and four huge tropical eagles (ecologically, this category could

---

> . . . to understand what kinds of eagles exist, we can now leave behind the constant revisions of taxonomy and look at the different niches, habits, and appearances of the birds we call "eagle."

---

include two of the booted eagles as well). The others are less classifiable. We should probably include three more species, all called eagle until recently and related to the ones above: the bateleur ("bateleur eagle"), a snake eagle; the eagle-buzzard (a South American bird formerly known as the buzzard-eagle); and the palm-nut vulture, a sea eagle relative formerly known as the vulturine fish eagle, which eats only palm nuts.

Sea Eagles

There are ten (or, if you count the palm-nut vulture, eleven) species of sea or fish eagles, forming a distinct natural and visual group. They are large to huge, big-billed and ponderous, usually have large patches of white feathers, and rarely stray from water. Sea eagles include one of the largest eagles in the world, the Steller's; one of the two best known (the iconic American bald eagle, symbol of the United States); and perhaps the best-studied eagle, the African fish eagle.

---

12 James Ferguson-Lees & David Christie. *Raptors of the World* (Boston, 2001). The author counted all species with "eagle" in the name.

Biologically, sea eagles are related to kites, especially the whistling and Brahminy kites, the last of which looks like a small sea eagle, complete with white head. All depend on fish to a greater or smaller extent. The large members of the group—bald, Steller's, and Eurasian white-tailed eagle—live far enough north that ice closes off their access to fish, and all supplement their diet with such things as ducks, seabirds, and carrion, especially that of marine mammals.

Louis Agassiz Fuertes painted this head of a juvenile Bald eagle.
Louis Agassiz Fuertes and the Singular Beauty of Birds, F. G. Marcham (ed.)

The Steller's eagle has the most massive bill of any eagle, and is one of the largest. ANIAD/SHUTTERSTOCK.COM

The African fish eagle is one of the most visible and best-studied species.
GEORGE W. CALEF

The Steller's sea eagle of the Russian Far East, Kamchatka, and the islands north of Japan, is one of the biggest of all the eagles, weighing up to nineteen pounds (nine kilograms).[13] It has a bill like a cleaver, apparently an adaptation for cutting through the thick skin and blubber of whale and sea elephant carcasses. While it takes advantage of salmon runs like all other sea eagles, it uses its size and power to prey upon quarry as large as full-grown geese.

---

13 Leslie Brown. *Eagles of the World* (New York, 1977), p. 48.

Also known as the Red-Backed Sea-Eagle, the Brahminy Kite has a wide range of habitats, and can be found from Sri Lanka to New South Wales, Australia. KITCH BAIN/SHUTTERSTOCK.COM

The palm nut "vulture" is an aberrant vegetarian eagle related to the sea eagles. JORDAN TAN/SHUTTERSTOCK.COM

The African fish eagle is as much a symbol of east and south African lakes as the bald eagle is of the United States. Every large body of water there holds its short-tailed, white-headed figure silhouetted atop a dead tree, soaring high or cruising low over the water, or calling with its head thrown back between its shoulders. Because its whole life cycle is visible in its open-country habitat, it bears the distinction of being the best-studied eagle in the world.

I will look at the bald eagle of North America throughout this book. After its numbers plummeted in the first three-quarters of the twentieth century from persecution, habitat loss, and the effects of DDT and other persistent pesticides, its population has rebounded. It even benefits from certain human-caused phenomena: Large congregations now gather in winter at Nankoweap Creek in the Grand Canyon, below Glen Canyon dam, to feed on concentrations of fish. Today it probably nests in closer association with human society than any other large eagle, and its numbers are expanding. It was removed from the Endangered Species list in 2006.

Mention should also be made of the odd palm-nut vulture. This tropical species resembles a sea eagle in every way, complete with a white head and strong talons. But according to the late Leslie Brown, it is "a unique, aberrant, mainly vegetarian bird of prey which subsists largely on the fatty pericap of oil-palm fruits."[14]

Snake Eagles

Snake eagles are superficially the least conventionally eaglelike of the birds we call eagles, unless we include, per recent suggestion, the immense Philippine eagle biologically in this group. (Even if we do, it belongs ecologically and visibly in the group of huge jungle eagles.) Snake eagles resemble buteos, harriers, and hawks. They range from small to medium in size and have (mostly) large yellow eyes, broad wings, and stout toes. They are common in the Old World tropics

---

14 Leslie Brown. *Eagles of the World* (New York, 1977), p. 19.

This small snake eagle is a typical member of the genus Spilornis.

and subtropics, absent from the Americas and (oddly) Australia. As most are entirely dependent on snakes for food, they cannot exist in high latitudes or at high altitudes, although one species, the short-toed eagle, nests in Southern Europe and up into Central Asia, where snakes abound in the hot dry summers (it migrates in winter.) Curiously, despite its appetite for venomous snakes, it has been persecuted in such places as France for centuries.

Their number is greatly increased in the genus *Spilornis* by a number of so-called "island endemics," individual species adapted in a classic Darwinian manner to the slightly differing habitats of the islands of Southeast Asia. In one instance, separate species even divide Borneo's habitat—one hunting in the mangroves at the sea's edge, the other in upland forests.[15]

---

15 Ferguson-Lees & Christie. *Raptors of the World*, p. 459.

The black-chested snake eagle is a typical member of the snake eagle genus. MARTIN MARITZ/SHUTTERSTOCK.COM

A young bateleur eagle shows off his facial ruff.
KEVIN BROWNE/BIGSTOCK.COM

Most snake eagles are rather similar except for size and plumage. The exception is the unique and magnificent bateleur of sub-Saharan Africa, the "flying wing" that dominates its skies. Bateleurs resemble no other bird. They have immense wings, an owl-like cowl around their bare red faces, and almost no tail. They whiz through the skies without flapping at speeds of sixty kilometers an hour, rocking from side to side, covering the distance from horizon to horizon in what seems like a moment on their long, leaf-shaped swept-back wings. Unlike other snake eagles, which just eat snakes, they gorge on everything from carrion to birds and mammals as well. They sun themselves with wings braced, facing the light, to restore feathers stressed by daylong high-speed soaring.[16] But despite their oddity, their feet, facial disks, and DNA indicate that they are snake eagle relatives.

Jungle Eagles

The huge jungle eagles form an obvious but probably artificial group based more on habitat, prey, and size than "blood" relationship. There are four big bare-legged eagles that may represent as many as three evolutionary groups, plus two very large booted eagles with similar habits.

The Philippine eagle (Pithecophaga jeffreyi), formerly inelegantly called the "monkey-eating eagle," may be related to the snake eagles and is one of the largest and the rarest eagles in the world. The New Guinea eagle (Harpyopsis nuovaeguineae) is an accipiter-like giant that may be related to kites. The legendary South American harpy (Harpia harpyia) may be the largest of all (as much as five kilograms); its smaller but still large relative, the crested eagle (Morphnus guianiensis) inhabits the same range, eating slightly smaller mammals and birds. These two may be allied to buteo hawks. The two booted eagles are African: the crowned eagle (Stephanoaetus coronatus) and the martial

---

16 Josep del Hoyo, Andrew Elliot, & Jordi Satagel, eds. Handbook of Birds of the World, vol. II (Barcelona, 1994), p. 132.

eagle *(Polemaetus bellicosus)*. Both are very large and probably related to the aquila eagles and, even more closely, to the smaller hawk eagles.

All of these birds but the martial eagle are ferocious predators of mammals up to the size of antelopes, including tree kangaroos, monkeys, and sloths, depending on where they live. The martial eagle occasionally kills antelopes but despite its size prefers game birds; it has the long wings characteristic of an open-country bird. All the others prefer closed-canopy forest and are built like accipiters, with short wings and long tails. We will revisit their methods in "Hunting Strategies."

Critically endangered, there may be as few as 180 individual Philippine eagles surviving in the wild. Edwin Verin/Shutterstock.com

A martial eagle, photographed in Kruger National Park, feeds on a rabbit. Riaan van den Berg/Shutterstock.com

The long-crested eagle of Africa is one of the "odd" eagles. John Baker/
Bigstock.com

Odd Eagles

There is a small number of what we might call "odd" eagles. Three of these are simply large birds of prey that show no obvious affinities with other groups. But one, the Indian black eagle *(Ictinaetus malayensis)*, is truly strange. While it superficially resembles a booted or aquila eagle, with feathered legs and a handsome profile, it has unusually large wings, described as "paddle shaped" in *Raptors of the World*,[17] that extend beyond the tips of its unusually long tail when folded, as well as weak feet with straight-tipped toes. Apparently these are modifications for acquiring the contents of birds' nests. We will examine this eagle's habits in more detail under "Hunting Strategies."

Booted Eagles

The rest of the eagles form a large natural group of birds with feathered legs and fierce predatory habits. They can be divided into two groups: "hawk eagles," which have, generally, shorter wings and long tails and hunt in forests and mixed country like big goshawks, and the long-winged open-country aquilas.

The hawk eagles of the genera *Spizaetus* and *Hieraaetus* include the smallest of all eagles, the pigeon-size and aptly named little eagle *(Hieraaetus morphnoides)* of Australia and New Guinea, as well as many large and powerful hunters like the Japanese *kumataka* (mountain hawk eagle, *Spizaetus nipalensis)*. Several of these eagles sport spiky crests like World War I German army helmets. All, even the little eagle, are bold and dynamic flyers capable of taking prey, both feathered and furred, larger than themselves, and several have been flown in traditional falconry in Europe, India, and Japan. One recently extinct member of the group, New Zealand's *Harpagornis moorei*, is now considered to be closely related to the *Hieraaetus* eagles. As it was the largest of all eagles (and quite possibly preyed on humans), it is amusing that its relative, the little eagle, is the smallest.[18]

---

17 Ferguson-Lees & Christie. *Raptors of the World*, p. 722.
18 Worthy and Holdaway. *Lost World of the Moa*, p. 722.

The *Aquila* group is considered a distinct genus, although some species have been switched back and forth between it and *Hieraaetus*. It contains a mix of smaller, rodent-eating species like the inoffensive lesser spotted eagle *(Aquila pomarina)*, slightly larger pirates like the tawny *(Aquila rapax)*, and bold aerial hunters like the golden itself.

The golden eagle *(Aquila chrysaetos)* is the quintessential capital-E eagle, the Platonic ideal of a bird of prey, and the one that gives its English name to the whole group. It is one of the world's most successful predators, found in most of the Northern Hemisphere. It ranges from the tundra to Mexico, North Africa, and northern India

---

The golden eagle *(Aquila chrysaetos)* is the
quintessential capital-E eagle, the Platonic ideal
of a bird of prey . . .

---

and hunts over forests and plain, mountain and desert. It is an important predator in Scotland, Siberia, and the Rocky Mountains. Its range of prey species is perhaps the broadest of all eagles: It has been recorded eating everything from carrion and beetles to pronghorn antelope, red deer, and calves.

In the Balkans it specializes in tortoises; in the forests of northeastern North America it hunts over bogs and, at least in summer, preys mostly on young bitterns and herons. In the western United States and in passes through Asian mountains, it preys on migrating cranes; its killing of reintroduced endangered whooping cranes put an end to one experimental program. In Gotland, off Sweden, it mostly consumes hedgehogs.

A hawk-eagle shows a characteristic spike-like crest.
BIRDS OF PREY BY JOSEPH WOLF

The golden is a typical aquila on the larger end of the scale. Small males (males are always smaller than females) can weigh six pounds; big Asian females, trained in falconry to hunt wolves, weigh nearly twenty. Golden eagles have large bills, more gracefully shaped than those of sea eagles; long shapely necks with a cape of "golden" hackle feathers on the nape; bulky bodies of chocolate brown or near black; long feathered wings; thick feathered legs: and thick feet with recurved talons. Young eagles, up to four years of age, have white patches at the

Fuertes' Golden eagle has attained its adult plumage.
Birds of America (New York, NY, 1917)

base of their primary wing feathers and black tipped white tails, the feathers of which are prized by cultures around the globe.

I somewhat romantically described my first encounter with a trained Kazakh eagle in Mongolia in my book *Eagle Dreams:*

> She looked as big as a sturdy human dwarf: thick,
> broad-shouldered, dark as a storm cloud. Her
> curving bill was horn, her feet shining yellow stone;

Juvenile and adult eagles often differ in color or markings. Here, the adult is on the right. GEORGE W. CALEF

The lesser spotted eagle often eats frogs.

BIRDS OF PREY BY JOSEPH WOLF

her gnarled knuckles bigger than mine, her two-inch claws a dragon's; a dinosaur's. Pale fluff fanned out over the white bases of her tail feathers. She stood relaxed, her talons spread over the top of a tractor's tire at the height of my waist so that her head nearly topped mine. Her braided leash connected the heavy sheepskin bracelets on her feathered legs to the hub of the wheel. From her left shoulder sprang a tuft, a plume of cloudy feathers as insubstantial as the river trees had seemed in the dawn. And she was perfect, with feathers as edged and shining as metal . . . In the bright desert light, she glowed like a dark sun, as elegant as a living thing can be. She was worth travelling four thousand miles to see.

Romantic, perhaps, but as we will see, aquila has impressed many cultures.

Not all aquilas are quite so, to use a loaded human term, "noble." As mentioned, some of the smaller ones conquer rodents at best, and the spotted eagles are not above catching frogs. The smallest, Wahlberg's eagle *(Aquila wahlbergi)* is an active predator like the smaller *Hieraaetus* eagles. But most of the large ones are formidable; even if, like the graceful wedged-tailed eagle of Australia, they are prone to scavenging carrion, they are capable of taking such things as medium-size kangaroos.

One aquila, the black, or Verreaux's, eagle of southern Africa, is an absolute specialist. Although it is superficially very much like the golden in size, proportion, and bold hunting style, and able on rare occasion to take large quarry, it usually confines its diet to little more than rock hyraxes, those strange marmotlike relatives of the elephant.

THE EAGLE'S EYE

From *Log-Book of a Fisherman and Zoologist;* Frank Buckland, 1875

The eagle is admirably adapted to perform the duties assigned to him. The anatomy of the eye of the eagle is in itself a study, and this wonderful organ has a power of vision, of which we men have not the slightest idea, even though our sight might be aided by a telescope.

The brain is large and well developed, the convolutions of grey matter dipped deep down into the white matter, thus showing a considerable amount of intelligence in the bird. The optic nerve is large, the coats of the eye strong and horny, but not so strong as the eyeballs of sharks and deep-water fish, which require a very tough coat (sclerotic) to the eye to stand the pressure of the water. The lens of the eagle's eye is very peculiar; it is flattened on each side and as brilliant as a diamond. A fish's lens is round. The eagle has, I believe, a muscular apparatus connected with his eye, by means of which he can convert it, as it were, into a telescope for seeing long distances, and he can so adapt his powers of vision as to see clearly at shorter distances. An eagle must have the most perfect organs of sight of any created thing. When he is soaring so high in the air that he can hardly be seen by the human eye, it is said the noble bird can see a hare or a lamb on the ground. I do not know of any good case where the sight of an eagle has been tested by experiment. The poor things are so hunted and persecuted, and the gun-bearing people are so anxious to destroy them, that they have no time or thought for experiment.

The black eagle looks predatory but eats mostly the contents of birds' nests. NICO SMIT/BIGSTOCK.COM

Hunting Strategies

With such a wide range of foods, eagles' hunting methods are equally varied, ranging from searching from the heights of a soar to passive watching from perches. Steppe and spotted eagles may even wander on the ground, picking up grasshoppers and beetles.

Fish eagles, whether employing either of the flight methods above, have a characteristic strike—approaching the surfacing fish with talons outstretched ahead and then hooking sharply back and down at the perigee of the swoop. Of course when salmon runs produce windrows of dead and dying salmon on the banks of rivers in Siberia and North America, there is no need for such strenuous acrobatics. Then crowds of eagles wade in the shallows, squabbling and squalling and standing around replete with bulging crops as bears fish between them and flocks of gulls scrabble for the scraps.

Although they are perfectly happy to eat fish, dead or alive, sea eagles are also formidable hunters of wildfowl. Bald and white-tailed eagles will harass ducks and divers on the water until the quarry is winded and unable to dive, then pluck it from the surface. Bald eagles have even been seen cruising in wave troughs, only to slip over the crest to pounce on seabirds floating on the other side.

Steppe eagles often walk on the ground in pursuit of rodents or insects.
Bratislav Grubac

The African fish eagle is also a specialized predator on the immense flocks of flamingos that breed and feed in the shallow soda lakes of the Rift Valley. Large young flamingos have no defense except to try to bury themselves in the flock; they cannot yet fly, and the lakes are too shallow for them to dive.

Sea eagles are also notorious "kleptoparasites"—thieves or pirates of other birds' kills. The classic instance is the American bald eagle's relentless harassment of the fish-eating osprey, or fish hawk *(Pandion*

Bald eagles will often congregate around plentiful food sources.
Uryadnikov Sergey/Shutterstock.com

haliaetus), an eaglelike bird that unlike the sea eagles is entirely dependent on fish. According to Mark Stalmaster in volume 4 of the *Handbook of North American Birds:*

> The eagle closes in below on a fish-carrying Osprey,
> forcing it to fly higher and higher. The osprey tries
> to keep above its tormentor, and, of course, the
> fish, when released from a greater altitude, is longer
> in falling. The fish is dropped, and the eagle tries
> —usually successfully—to catch it during its fall.
> Nicholson (1952) may have been the first to describe
> 2 eagles cooperatively attacking an osprey; 1 eagle
> turned belly-up and took the fish from its captor.[19]

Snake eagles do not need to be particularly agile; most hunt from lookout perches or hover above their prey like great kestrels. They use their short, stout toes to grasp their writhing quarry and puff out their feathers to deflect strikes, for they are not immune to venom.

Jungle eagles may hunt by cutting through the canopy, like goshawks, to surprise monkeys or to pluck sloths like hairy fruit, but they also sit on perches and listen. All have crests and elaborate facial feathering, and the harpy has facial disks like an owl. Owls use these disks to direct sound to their asymmetrical ear openings, which make it possible for them to pinpoint sounds more exactly than other animals. Harpies apparently do not have the different ear shapes that owls do, but they do make more use of their ears than most other birds. Harvard researcher Alberto Palleroni played tapes of various sounds, including howler monkey (a prey species), tinamous (a neutral species), and pure tones, as well as sounds of other harpies, to experienced hunting birds and inexperienced captives.[20] Differences in response indicated

---

19 Ralph Palmer, ed. *Handbook of North American Birds*, vol. IV, p. 229.
20 Alberto Palleroni & Marc Hauser. "Experience-Dependent Plasticity for Auditory Processing in a Tropical Raptor," *Science*, vol. 229 (2003) pp. 1195–96.

that hunting experience had caused a neurological change. "for naïve harpies, howlers elicit the same kind of orienting response as do tinamous and pure tones, whereas for experienced harpies, howler calls elicit the same kind of orienting response as do harpy contact calls. Neither age nor familiarity can explain these results because the naïve and experienced harpies overlap in age and all birds have heard howler calls throughout their lives." It would be interesting to know if other forest eagles share similar responses.

The unique Indian black eagle is adapted to hunt for its peculiar diet, mostly birds' eggs and nestlings. It cruises at canopy height on forest hillsides in mountainous country up to twenty-five hundred meters above sea level, searching for its passive prey. According to Brown and Amadon:

> . . . it soars in a peculiar manner, moving always at very slow pace, with the wings held out at full stretch and rather above the back, the primaries very widely separated and projecting some distance from the wing-tip . . . it shows extraordinary ability to fly at a slow pace, and to circle in and out of small bays in the forest, just above the tree-tops.
>
> There seems little doubt that the peculiar very long and soft primaries must be an adaptation to assist the very slow mode of flight, which is of use to the bird in its minute search of forest and grassy hillsides for birds' nests . . . the flexibility and great length of the primaries would permit of exceptionally wide separation at the tips, which could be a useful adaptation enabling the bird to maintain very low flying speeds.[21]

---

21 Leslie Brown & Dean Amadon. *Eagles, Hawks, and Falcons of the World* (Seacaucus, NJ, 1989), p. 642.

As some might expect, the widest range of techniques and prey is found in the booted eagles. Golden eagle researcher Jeff Watson breaks down hunting methods in that species into seven categories plus carrion eating; they probably cover all the possibilities in the entire booted group. They include "High soar with glide attack", "High soar with a vertical stoop", "Contour flight with short glide attack", "Glide attack with tail chase", "Low flight with slow descent attack", "Low flight with sustained grip attack" (this is the technique eagles use to kill large mammals), and "Walk and grab attack."[22]

Some of these, like the last, amount to grazing, but some are spectacular. The "High soar with vertical stoop," which I have witnessed, resembles the power dive of a peregrine falcon made by a bird six to twelve times as large, hurtling down from the sky in an inverted heart shape to strike a bird from the air like a feathered thunderbolt. Goldens usually use the technique on large birds like geese or sage grouse, but African martial eagles will fall from a great height to kill large mammals like antelope as well.

Golden eagles are extremely specialized in habitats where their choices are restricted. In Greece and parts of the Balkans (and perhaps other dry lands near the Mediterranean) eons of land abrasion by grazing have degraded the habitat and reduced available prey species to tortoises (and perhaps unprotected lambs). Golden eagles in these locales therefore eat mostly tortoises, which they have learned to carry aloft and drop onto stone in order to crack them open. Traditionally the death of the Greek dramatist Aeschylus in 456 BC was attributed to an eagle; the anecdote relates that an eagle dropped a tortoise on Aeschylus's bald head, killing him![23] Modern revisionists have suggested that the culprit was a lammergeier (bearded vulture), but as these birds are more likely to drop bones than turtles, the Greeks were probably correct.

---

22 Jeff Watson. *The Golden Eagle* (London 1997) p. 48.
23 Watson. *The Golden Eagle*, p. 264.

However, when large animals are available, golden eagles have little difficulty switching to such food sources, which may last them for weeks. As it is impossible for an eagle to carry prey much larger than a hare, eagle parents rarely attack the biggest quarry when they are raising young. But in winter they are surprisingly bold. In our age of environmental awareness, conservationists sometimes claim that all

Golden eagles can be quite specialized in their preferred prey, depending upon their habitat. In this famous 1924 painting by Bruno Liljefors, a golden pursues a hare. WIKICOMMONS

> . . . all authoritative modern scientific books on
> eagles and specifically golden eagles "credit" them
> with the ability to occasionally kill full-size deer and
> antelope, especially in winter.

traditional accounts of eagle killing hoofed game are suspect. But in fact all authoritative modern scientific books on eagles and specifically golden eagles "credit" them with the ability to occasionally kill full-size deer and antelope, especially in winter. (I know a biologist in Wyoming who witnessed a single female take down a pronghorn antelope.) Anthropologist George Frison, who spent a lifetime in the field there, gives a vivid account:

> On two different occasions in late winter, I witnessed
> weakened pronghorn killed by pairs of golden eagles.
> Both times, one eagle flew over the animal to distract
> it while the second one lit on the animal's back and
> ripped open the hide. They both began to consume
> the exposed flesh before the animal died. Other
> eagles soon joined the first two; within a few hours,
> little remained except head, bones, feet, and a few
> scraps rapidly being eaten or carried away by ravens
> and magpie. The late William Maycock, a long-time
> hunter and outfitter in eastern Wyoming, observed an
> almost identical occurrence, and, having considerable
> artistic talent, he painted a picture of the event.[24]

---

24 George Frison. *Surviving by Hunting* (Berkeley and Los Angeles, 2004), p. 25.

These predatory attacks and defensive maneuvers of the eagle and fish hawk are matters of daily observation along the whole of our seaboard, from Georgia to New England, and frequently excite great interest in the spectators. Sympathy, however, generally sides with the honest and laborious sufferer in opposition to the attacks of power, injustice, and rapacity—qualities for which our hero is so generally notorious and in which his superior, man, are equally detestable. As for the feelings of the poor fish, they seem altogether out of the question.

Love and Death Among the Eagles

Many eagles have spectacular "epigamic," or nuptial, ceremonies. These vary from calling loudly from an exposed perch, through soaring and undulating flight, and culminate in the locked-talon displays of some fish eagles. Of calling duets, Leslie Brown wrote of the African fish eagle that they " . . . begin calling about every forty minutes before sunrise, the first calls immediately stimulate other pairs to 'sing,' and for a few minutes the whole shore rings with glorious sound. They then

Steppe eagle eggs. BRATISLAV GRUBAC

THE BALD EAGLE

From *The Living World: A Complete Natural History of the World's Creatures, Fishes, Reptiles, Insects, Birds and Mammals*; J. W. Buel, 1889

This bird has long been known to naturalists, being common to both continents, and occasionally met with from a very high northern latitude to the borders of the torrid zone, but chiefly in the vicinity of the sea, and along the shores and cliffs of our lakes and large rivers. Formed by nature for braving the severest cold; feeding equally on the produce of the sea and of the land; possessing powers of flight capable of outstripping even the tempests themselves; unawed by anything but man; and from the ethereal heights to which he soars, looking abroad, at one glance, on an immeasurable expanse of forests, fields, lakes of seasons, as, in a few minutes, he can pass from summer to winter, from the lower to the higher regions of the atmosphere, the abode of eternal cold, and from thence descend at will to the torrid or the arctic regions of the earth. He is therefore found at all seasons in the countries he inhabits, but prefers all such places as have been mentioned above, from the great partiality he has for fish. In procuring these, he displays, in a very singular manner, the genius and energy of his character, which is fierce, contemplative, daring, and tyrannical; attributes not exerted but on particular occasions; but when put forth, overpowering all opposition. Elevated on the high dead limb of some gigantic tree that commands a wide view of the neighboring shore and ocean, he seems calmly to contemplate the motions of the various feathered tribes that pursue their bust avocations below; the snow-white gulls slowly winnowing the air; the busy tringa (sand-pipers) coursing along the sands; trains of ducks streaming over the surface; silent and watchful cranes, intent and wading; clamorous crows, and all the winged multitudes that subsist by the bounty of this vast liquid magazine of nature. High over all these hovers one whose action instantly arrests all attention. By his wide curvature of wing, and sudden suspension in the air, he knows him to be the fish hawk (*Pandion haliaetus*) settling over some devoted victim of the deep. His eye kindles at the sight, and balancing himself, with half-opened wings, on the branch, he watches the result. Down, rapid as an arrow from heaven, descends the distant object of his attention, the roar of its wings reaching the ear as it disappears in the deep, making the surge foam around. At this moment the eager looks of the eagle are all ardor, and leveling his neck for flight, he sees the fish hawk once more emerge, struggling with his prey, and mounting the air with screams of exultation. These are the signal for our hero, who launching into the air, instantly gives chase, and soon gains on the fish hawk; each exerts his utmost to mount above the other, displaying in the rencontre the most elegant and sublime aerial evolutions. The unencumbered eagle rapidly advances, and is just on the point of reaching his opponent, with a sudden scream, probably of despair and honest execration, the latter dumps his fish; the eagle poising himself for a moment as if to take a more certain aim, descends like a whirlwind, snatches it in his grasp ere it reaches the water, and bears his ill-gotten booty silently away to the woods . . .

A steppe eagle broods on her ground nest in Mongolia.
Bratislav Grubac

fly to fishing posts where they readily call in challenge to a neighbour, or the passage of another fish eagle or even an aeroplane overhead."[25] Many species of sea eagles are vocal and loud—the African's scientific name is appropriately *Haliaeetus vocifer.*

Martial eagles soar and call; crowned eagles call and fly in undulating paths, diving and soaring. Golden eagles do the same but silently, perhaps because they inhabit more open country where they can be more easily seen. Verrauxs do the same but with higher dives of up to one thousand feet. Goldens also call and touch talons, with one participant upside down.

These displays culminate in the locked-talon spinning-wheel displays of sea eagles. Leslie Brown has a vivid description: "The last form of display, whirling or spinning, is apparently the most intense. In this, the two eagles, after soaring together for some time, or after mutual

---

25 Brown. *Eagles of the World,* p. 126.

The bateleur in flight resembles a "flying wing" and covers huge territories at high speed. Johan Swanepoel/Bigstock.com

calling and foot touching displays, lock their claws to one another and either come whirling down wing over wing in a series of cartwheels, or, facing one another, spin laterally and fall more gently earthwards. In either case the effect is extremely spectacular." The American poet Walt Whitman commemorated such displays in a poem called "The Dalliance of the Eagles."

Golden eagles usually nest high on cliffs. George W. Calef

Imperial eagles build typical stick nests in trees. BRATISLAV GRUBAC

After display and mating comes nest building or, since eagle nests may last for years or even decades, nest repair and refurbishing. As Brown says, "Eagles' nests are traditionally large or enormous and occupied for many years." I have lived in rural New Mexico for nearly thirty years, and the nearest golden eagle nest, an immense stick structure in a hollow in the side of a nearby mountain, has been active and constantly replenished for all that time; theoretically it could have been so for centuries or even millennia. Of course eagles are not that long-lived; they mate for life, but "widows" quickly pick up new mates from the floating population of young unmated birds, so nest occupation is continuous. Sea and fish eagles, jungle eagles, and all booted eagles build such large semipermanent structures whether in trees or on cliff ledges. All the snake eagles but the always-contrary bateleur build smaller, single-season stick nests like hawks.

These chicks of the imperial eagle were photographed in Serbia.
BRATISLAV GRUBAC

Female eagles are larger than males, the universal condition among raptors. Such differences are greater when the prey is large and energetic, smaller when the prey is small or when food is carrion (as in vultures) or inactive. The difference apparently opens up a greater range of prey to exploitation, with the female taking such things as large mammals while the more agile male hunts swift birds. The female needs her bulk to produce eggs, and her larger size may help her defend the nest. (Falconers have long recognized such reversals of human stereotypes. Males are considered more nervous and emotional; females stronger, more aggressive, and dominant.)

... eagles are not that long-lived; they mate for life, but "widows" quickly pick up new mates from the floating population of young unmated birds ...

In the behavioral trait called "Cainism," the larger chick kills and eats the smaller. BRATISLAV GRUBAC

The nesting site of a steppe eagle. BRATISLAV GRUBAC

Both sexes of eagles care for the young and, once the eaglets need no shelter from the mother, bring and carefully "process" food, ripping it up and offering bits until the eaglets can feed themselves. Eagles may lay one, two, three, or rarely four eggs. But in many or even most species, only one young bird will survive. Sea eagles seem less aggressive, but in most other eagles, the first chick to hatch gets a head start. When the second chick hatches a day or two later, the first will begin to peck and bully it. Soon the firstborn will either kill the younger bird or drive it to the edge of the nest, where it will soon die of exposure and neglect, at which point the firstborn will eat it. The parents never interfere, and the submissive second chick is too intimidated to even beg for food. Approximately 30 to 40 percent of all eagles hatched succumb to this so-called "Cainism," named for the biblical Cain who murdered his brother.

It was once thought that such killings were caused by lack of food, but they occur in the vast majority of eagle broods, even in times of abundance. It was also thought that the first was usually the larger female, but the sex of the first chick is utterly random, and such an imbalanced ratio would soon have led to a severe shortage of males. Apparently all eggs beyond the first are merely insurance policies against the first's being infertile. Some species, like the crowned eagle, have never been recorded raising more than one chick, but even among small inoffensive aquilas, a surviving second is a rare phenomenon.

Migration

Only eleven species of eagles migrate. Of these, one, the Wahlberg's eagle, migrates north from southern Africa; the others are typical Northern Hemisphere winter migrants. In some species like the golden, arctic populations are more likely to migrate than southern, and immature, white-marked yearlings are more migratory than breeders of four and more years. Where I live, the stay-at-home breeders are besieged each winter by legions of migrant young with white, black-tipped tails. The

The graceful Wahlberg's eagle is one of the smallest of the true booted eagles. STEPHENE/SHUTTERSTOCK.COM

residents are dominant and often drive the yearlings off roadkill deer or pound them out of the air with dazzling dives and strikes.

Eagles migrate by alternately soaring up on rising thermal currents and gliding forward until they are low, then catching another thermal and rising again. In North America migrant eagles, especially goldens, follow the air currents generated by the Rocky Mountain chain in the west and the Appalachians in the east. In modern times scientists place trapping and banding stations at well-known narrow spots in the mountains, like the Sandia Mountains over Albuquerque in New Mexico or at Hawk Mountain in Pennsylvania, where thousands of hawks and eagles once were shot.

Because thermals don't work over water, great concentrations of booted, snake, and aquila eagles stack up at narrow chokepoints to cross water at Gibraltar, Suez, and the Bosporus. They also filter through Himalayan passes, along with geese and cranes that may become prey. Around the Mediterranean many are still killed for sport at these bottlenecks, a phenomenon we will examine at greater length in "The Future of Eagles."

Eagles, especially bald eagles, also wander in fall and winter in search of rich sources of food. These rather sociable birds can sometimes appear in huge flocks at places like Homer, Alaska, and Nankoweap Creek in the Grand Canyon. These concentrations can become great tourist attractions, with trees and beaches festooned with hundreds of spectacular white-headed birds.

The steppe eagle is one of the species that migrate around the Mediterranean. BRATISLAV GRUBAC

CHAPTER 2

EAGLES OF THE MIND: MYTHOLOGY, ART, AND POPULAR CULTURE

"He is thus closely associated with the Sun god and in fact often appears to fly to the Sun's home above the visible sky."

—Pueblo Myth

One hundred kilometers north of the city of Almaty in Kazakhstan, on the endless windy steppes that stretch from the towering Tian Shan range in the south for hundreds of miles north to the forests of Siberia, a low, rounded range of black volcanic rock breaks the horizon. Its canyon walls bear the imprint of hundreds of petroglyphs, a palimpsest of rock art figures dating from as far back as 1600 BC up to the nineteenth century. Realistic images of animals mingle with charioteers, sun-headed gods, erotic figures, and lines of dancers.

The petroglyph at Tamgaly in Kazakhstan shows the early association of human, horse, hound, and eagle. STEPHEN BODIO

Among them is an amazing image usually dated to about 1300 to 1200 BC,[26] a time when the most realistic animal depictions dominate. It is not only among the earliest eagle images known but also unites the eagle with its hunting partners today: humans, dogs, and horses. It is no accident that here, in the plains north of the Tian Shan, the earliest archaeological sites of horse domestication unite with some of the earliest tracks of canine DNA and the earliest evidence of falconry.

In the petroglyph a large prey beast, variously identified as an onager or wild ass (which I believe) or a female red deer, stands besieged by two ring-tailed hounds similar to the primitive Russian laikas of today. A saddled horse waits in the background, while a human stands in front of the quarry, ready to aid his allies as he would today.

---

26 Renato Sala. Personal communication.

The association of eagle and falconer in Central Asia has not changed in thousands of years. DAVID EDWARDS

A petroglyph from Kochkor, in Kyrgizstan, dated about AD 600, shows a falconer carrying his eagle. RENATO SALA, LAB GEOARCHAEO; ALMATY, KAZAKHSTAN

On the back of the prey stands a figure I identify as an eagle. One respected archaeologist friend thinks it is another dog.[27] But what dog would stand on the back of its quarry, facing the tail? Both dogs are depicted as they would actually be—ring-tailed and baying at the head of the onager. (Other petroglyphs depict realistic wolves with tails held low, visibly different from the dogs, which are always depicted with tails up.) The figure at the back has no tail at all.

Interestingly, every falconer to whom I have shown this image has immediately, without prompting, identified it as I do. And another archaeologist has changed his interpretation when I showed him photos of eagles with large quarry. Nor is the size of prey a deterrent;

---

27 Renato Sala. Personal communication.

as will be seen in the next chapter, Kazakh and Kirghiz falconers still hunt roe deer, red deer, saiga antelope, and even wolves with their eagles. (Onagers are now endangered or extinct in the homelands of eagle falconry.)

Eagles in Mythology

The petroglyph appears to modern eyes as a realistic description of hunting partners, though one serious enough to be carved in stone. But images of eagles immediately breed multiple meanings. Eagles became symbols of good and evil, religious metaphors, even gods. Ambiguity is inherent in a creature being revered and admired for its power but feared and hated for its ferocity and because it preys on game and herd animals that "belong" to humans. The old rock painting looks to us like "art." But are religious depictions of the "Eagle of Woe" in the Apocalypse also art? What about eagles as military symbols or national emblems, eagles on money or stamps, eagles as mascots for sporting teams? I hope to follow a winding, branching trail through all of these holy eagles and eagle symbols, finally returning to eagles in art and literature and popular culture. It is a long road.

Eagles still have a mythic resonance in the lands of the Asian eagle hunters—Mongolia, southern Siberia, Kazakhstan, Turkmenistan, Kyrgyzstan. Many of the people there are nominally Moslem but deeply animist and shamanist, giving only lip service to Islam. According to Konstantonov, Lebedev, and Malouichko's *Birds in Folklore, Myths, Legends and Peoples Names,* the word for "golden eagle" (berkuts, bircut, burgud) is similar in Russian, Ukranian, Mongolian, Turkic, Tatarian, and Polish. What's more, it is allied to "father" (berkut-baba) and even "God." "In the pre-Islamic mythology of the Turcomans— 'Burkut-divana' means 'Burkut-highest God,' host of the skies, lightning, and rain, equal in status to Allah himself."

The native peoples of Siberia also revere the eagle. In the mythology of the Yenisei, Ostyaks, Teleuts, Orochons, and other Siberian peoples, it is believed that the first shaman was born of an eagle or learned his arts from one.[28] Drawings of eagles and eagle-feather costumes are part of the shaman's kit even today. For instance, the headgear of a Tuvan shaman consists of forty large and twenty small eagle feathers, with each quill wrapped in soft leather and fixed to a cap.

The Turukhansk Yakuts considered the eagle to be the creator of the first shaman and also the creator of light. Its children were represented as spirit birds sitting in the branches of the Tree of the World, topped by a two-headed eagle, the master of the birds. (It is worth noting that to this day, the two-headed eagle is the symbol of Russia.) Yakuts still connect the eagle to sacred trees. Orochons consider it the progenitor of mankind.

> The Turukhansk Yakuts considered the eagle
> to be the creator of the first shaman and also
> the creator of light.

Buryats living near Lake Baikal believe the eagle to be the son of the "owner" of Olkhon Island, a terrifying deity living in a shaman cave there. Another Buryat legend says that kind gods sent the eagle to Earth to save humans from the intrigues of malicious spirits. The humans refused to believe him, so the eagle wedded a human woman. The first Buryat shaman, Mergen Jora, or Buheli Jara, was born of this woman.

It is an interesting feature of Central Asian mythology that eagles are virtually always benevolent, unlike their more equivocal good/powerful/evil status in many other cultures. Native Americans share a benevolent view of eagles; it is tempting to wonder if they brought such beliefs with them across the Bering Strait from Asia.

---

28 V. V. Ryabtsev & Jevgeni Shergalin (trans.). *Orly Baileala* (Irkutsk, 2000), pp. 11–15.

Virtually all North American tribes that know eagles have beliefs and legends about them. The tribes of Southern California believed that eagles could be messengers to the land of the dead.

> When a person died, people came from various
> villages to make a "death visit"; they brought gifts
> for the performance of a special ceremony, one of
> the most valued such gifts being a live bird: either a
> young Golden Eagle, a Bald (White-headed) Eagle,
> or a California Condor. This bird was raised in
> captivity until the time for the "Bird Feast" or "Eagle
> Killing" ceremony arrived. It was then taken to the
> sacred enclosure by the *paha*, whose ceremonial
> attire included either red and black or red, white, and
> black bodypaint and an eagle-feather skirt. The bird
> was strangled to death, care being taken to avoid
> shedding a single drop of its blood. The bird's carcass
> was skinned and its body buried within the sacred
> enclosure; the feathers were used in the costliest and
> most elaborate ritual paraphernalia or for decorating
> images of the dead.[29]

Among tribes there both the shape-changing element and the reverence for the eagle were explicit:

> One version of the origin of the ceremony stated
> that the god *Chinigchinich* instructed the Indians
> how to perform it, and that the bird had originally
> been a woman who had run off to the mountains
> and been transformed by that god. The sacrifice
> was thus performed so that she could assume her

---

29 Travis Hudson & Ernest Underhay. *Crystals in the Sky* (Santa Barbra, 1978), pp. 85–88.

human form once again and return to her mountain home. In contrast to this Juaneño-Luiseño view, the Grabrielino explained that a man upon his deathbed once requested that his people be given his feathers, since he was soon to be transformed into a bird. The Eagle Killing Ceremony was thus made not to honor a god, but rather to honor the memory of this man, for the people had great reverence for the eagle.[30]

These days most of these customs are no longer practiced, though many tribes still use eagle feathers in dances and ceremonies. (Native Americans are the only people allowed to possess eagle feathers and parts.) Others, like the tribes of the Pacific Northwest, still portray the bald eagle on totem poles, though they have little or no physical contact with the birds. But among one group, the Pueblo peoples of Arizona and New Mexico, there is a special relationship with eagles and a single tribe, the Hopi, who still keeps eagles and uses them in ceremonies.

Eagle myths of all kinds pervade Pueblo mythology, perhaps because in the high-mesa pueblos, humans have always lived alongside the eagle.[31] The inhabitants of Picuris Pueblo believe that Eagle once resembled a crow, but he told two boys searching for their parents that if they would paint his feathers he would take them up to where the sun lived. They painted his legs and beak yellow and his tail white with a black tip, like that of a young golden eagle, and he took them to the Sun's land, where they found their parents.

For the Keresan, eagles were associated with the clouds that brought the rains. For the Tewa, the eagle brought corn. Several pueblos, like the California tribes, believed in an association of the eagle with the dead. The Hopi thought that eagles were the natural foe of the rattlesnake. At Acoma (the "sky city" perched above the plains like an eagle's nest) the people thought that Eagle could cure

---

30 Hudson & Underhay. *Crystals in the Sky* (Santa Barbra, 1978), p. 88.
31 Hamilton A. Tyler. *Pueblo Birds and Myths* (Flagstaff, AZ, 1991), p. 49.

Some eagle totem poles still exist in the Pacific northwest of America.
AlexAranda/Shutterstock.com

the sick. And the Hopis believed in a monster eagle bigger than a man, which abducted women—legend or folk memory of the great eaglelike teratorns that might have survived to the time of the "first Americans"?

Despite the Pueblos' reverence for eagles, all tribes would sacrifice eagles by strangling them or smothering them in corn meal. Hopi practice, still followed today, is typical:

> On First and Third mesas at Hopi the eagle victim
> is buried in a special plot, but on Second Mesa there
> is a division of treatment as with human bodies.
> The bird is given a final meal of rabbit flesh so that
> its soul will have "ample strength to fly back to the
> buttes after death." Then it is either burned in fissures
> on the cliff, as are very young babies, or, if an adult

bird, the body is taken to the owner's cornfield. It is buried in the corn because, "the eagle is the most important animal friend of the Hopi and the old bird is like a grownup person."[32]

Eagles are still killed today by the Pueblos; I will examine the controversy in more detail in "Eagle as Enemies." But make no doubt about the reverence they have for eagles:

> Eagle is a friend because he protects the cornfield in a literal sense by destroying its pests and also by acting as the all-seeing eye that looks down as the Sun does from the sky and takes account of things done on earth. He is thus closely associated with the Sun god and in fact often appears to fly to the Sun's home above the visible sky.

Eagles are not as common in classical and Christian imagery as they are in the cultures of Asia and America, and they are often portrayed as either evil or merely powerful rather than benevolent. (This is also an argument against an early date for falconry in Europe and the Middle East—but as we shall see, there are many beautiful and realistic images of eagles in Far Eastern art.) The earliest eagle image cited in Francis Klingender's magisterial *Animals in Art and Thought to the End of the Middle Ages*,[33] a fairly Eurocentric book but one that goes back to the time of the cave paintings, is a fifth-century-BC Greek coin portraying an eagle attacking a hare.

The Egyptians used an eagle hieroglyphic to represent the soul. According to Watson[34] this symbol, looking like a perching eagle facing left, evolved into the letter "A," through the refinements of the

---

32 Tyler. *Pueblo Birds and Myths*, p. 49.
33 Francis Klingender. *Animals in Art and Thought* (Cambridge, MA, 1971), p. 70.
34 Jeff Watson. *The Golden Eagle*, p. 258.

COLLECTING DIAMONDS WITH EAGLES

From *The Travels of Marco Polo;* c. thirteenth century

Near the summit, it is said, there are deep valleys, full of caverns and surrounded by precipices, amongst which the diamonds are found; and here many eagles and white storks, attracted by the snakes on which they feed, are accustomed to make their nests. The persons who are in quest of the diamonds take their stand near the mouths of the caverns, and from thence cast down several pieces of flesh, which the eagles and storks pursue into the valley, and carry off with them to the tops of the rocks. Thither the men immediately ascend, drive the birds away, and recovering the pieces of meat, frequently find diamonds sticking to them. Should the eagles have had time to devour the flesh, they watch the place of their roosting at night, and in the morning find the stones amongst the dung and filth that drops from them. But you must not suppose that the good diamonds come among Christians, for they are carried to the grand khan, and to the kings and chiefs of that country.

Phoenician alphabet. "It was in fact the two eagle pictures on the Rosetta Stone, and the recognition that these represented the letter 'a' in the name 'Cleopatra,' that helped unlock the mystery of Egyptian hieroglyphic writing."

Eagles had a place in classical mythology and imagery. Zeus was often portrayed as an eagle and was alleged to have kidnapped the beautiful young Trojan prince Ganymede, the embodiment of male beauty, in the guise of an eagle. The incident has been depicted both

*Bertel Thorvaldsen created his own version of the Ganymede legend
sometime between 1817 and 1823.* Wikimedia

in lifelike sculptures and in an astonishingly ugly and unanatomical painting by Rubens.

Early biblical references to eagles are often admiring. In Genesis the Spirit of God "soared like an eagle" over the waters of creation. The quotation from Proverbs (" . . . the way of the eagle in the air; the way of a serpent on a rock; the way of a ship in the midst of the sea; the way of a man with a maiden . . . ") breathes wonder.

But most biblical and early Christian references paint the eagle in darker hues. They were listed first amongst the "unclean" birds that are prohibited to Jews as food. The Old Testament reads:

But these are they of which ye shall not eat: the eagle,
and the ossifrage and the osprey, and the glede, and
the kite, and the vulture after his kind, and every
raven after his kind, and the owl, and the night,
and the cuchow, and the hawk after his kind, the
little owl, and the great owl, and the swan, and the
pelican, and the geir eagle . . .

Klingender has an interesting theory that those "unclean" birds
were holy birds of earlier peoples: " . . . the unclean abominable beasts
and birds associated in orthodox Jewish thought and in the Book of
Revelation with devils, doleful creatures and foul spirits were scared
animals linked in some cases with the deities of the ancient oriental
religions and in others with more primitive rituals of the pre-Yawhedic
Jewish cult."

The great Christian eagle image became the "Eagle of Woe" of the
Apocalypse. A good example is in a magnificent illuminated volume
made for King Henry II between 1007 and 1010. Klingender describes
a pair of eagles ripping at two fallen kings there: "John and the angel
watch two birds dive down on two prostrate kings below. They alight
with beating wings, their claws poised to rend their victims, their eyes
set in barbaric scrolls. The birds are mighty eagles, of the same brood
as the eagle of woe looking back at John depicted earlier."[35]

Such imagery and such a dark reputation are the rule in the
Western tradition up through the popular art of the nineteenth
century, which we will look at later. While eagles continued to be fierce
martial symbols, from Rome to the United States, they rarely appeared
"benign"; in a culture without traditions of eagle falconry, eagles were
competitors rather than friends. Oddly, the one exception comes from
St. John. The four evangelists each had his symbol, and John's was

---

35 Klingender. *Animals in Art and Thought*, p. 225.

an eagle, symbolizing God's all-seeing eye. An additional meaning seems almost Native American; because in some ways John's gospel is considered "higher" than the other three, so the eagle soars above the terrestrial symbols of man, ox, and lion.

Banners, Flags, Mascots: Eagle Symbols

The ferocity, strength, and courage of eagles have made them symbols for armies, countries, and sports teams as long as such things have existed. The Roman legionary Aquila, real and as a symbolic start, traveled at the head of Caesar's armies. Double-headed eagles adorn the banners of the Habsburgs and the czars and have returned as a symbol of Russia since the fall of the Soviet Union. Reflecting the dark side of the symbolism, the eagle was also appropriated by the Nazis.

Eagles also abound in Central Asian national symbolism. An eagle adorns the seal of the Republic of Kyrgyzstan and is on the back of its money, as a character of the national epic, the *Manas*. Kazakhstan has a prominent eagle on its flag and has issued a stamp with—what else?—an eagle hunting over two tazis as a rider gallops behind; Kyrgyzstan has a similar one!

But the most ubiquitous and best-known eagle is the bald eagle symbol of the United States, with its iconic white head, known to friend and foe alike.

The species nearly lost the job before it started. Although already a symbol for both Native Americans (particularly in the totem poles

This stone incarnation can be seen on the Saint Angelo bridge in Rome.
FOTOECHO/SHUTTERSTOCK.COM

This Russian imperial eagle sits on the gate of the Winter Palace in Saint Petersburg. EUGENE SURGEEV/SHUTTERSTOCK.COM

of the Pacific Northwest) and in the colonies (an early Massachusetts penny), the eagle was not favored by the chairman of the committee to design the emblem for the "Great Seal," Benjamin Franklin, who disapproved of the bird's moral character (he preferred the turkey). The artist Audubon, who agreed, quoted him in his *Ornithological Biographies* (see sidebar "Against the Bald Eagle"):

> I wish the Bald Eagle had not been chosen the
> Representative of our Country. He is a Bird of
> bad moral Character. He does not get his Living
> honestly. . . .[36]

36 John James Audubon. *Writings and Drawings* (New York, 1999), p. 247.

This Nazi-era rendering of an eagle head by sculptor W. Lemke once stood on the top of a terminal at Berlin's Tempelhof Airport; a grim consideration of a noble bird. GARY BLAKELY/SHUTTERSTOCK.COM

A creature that so readily lends itself to symbolism and interpretation can unfortunately be appropriated and used for even the worst ends, as seen in this Nazi-era postage stamp. WIKIMEDIA

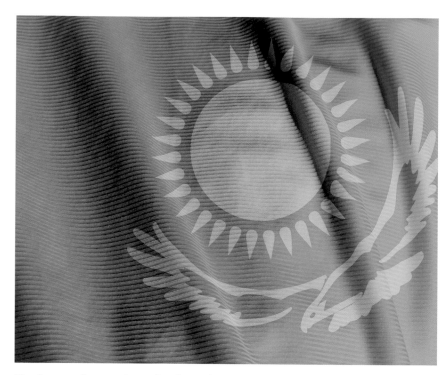

Eagles are featured on the flag of Kazakhstan . . .
MATT TROMMER/SHUTTERSTOCK.COM

*. . . The presidential seal of the
United States . . .*
LUMAXART/BIGSTOCK.COM

*. . . and on the now-obsolete silver
US Morgan dollar.*
RSOOLL/SHUTTERSTOCK.COM

On the Great Seal of the United States, the bird is depicted head-on, wings spread, holding the arrows of war in one foot and the olive branch of peace in the other. Various versions have appeared on coins, paper bills, and flags and as a symbol of the postal service. Its image, from realistic to cartoonish, may be among the best-known icons in the world. It has been used as a military symbol, as by the 101st Airborne Division, "The Screaming Eagles," and has been appropriated as a mascot of gun-safety education by the National Rifle Association ("Eddie Eagle").

An actual bald eagle, caught by a Chippewa and traded in 1861 to a Union artillery company, became a living mascot in the Civil War. Known as "Old Abe," he participated in forty-two battles and skirmishes, in one of which he had some of his tail feathers shot off. He lived until 1881 and was saluted by Gen. Ulysses S. Grant.

Countless sports teams also use the eagle as a symbol, though use of a living bald eagle is not allowed today. (Possession of the bird or any of its parts is illegal under federal law because it is a national symbol and, until recently, a protected species under the Endangered Species Act, both of which we will look at later.)

The last situation led to an act that I have never regretted, though I will leave out the name of the school. When I was at college one of the myriad teams that use eagles as mascots could not obtain a bald eagle and so bought a pair of tawny eagles. The two birds were badly fed and otherwise mistreated and were hauled out for half-time shows at football games by two fraternity oafs who forced them to flap and let them dangle from their fists. After one died of mishandling, the veterinarian of the zoo where they were kept helped me "disappear" the remaining bird to a breeding project while alleging it too had died, "of a broken heart." Alas, such things would probably not be possible in today's world of paperwork.

The image is associated with the United States by others as well, and not necessarily by the country's fans. An Al Jazeera cartoon of 2004 first shows an Arab falconer innocently hunting then shows images of

AGAINST THE BALD EAGLE

An excerpt from a letter written by Benjamin Franklin to his daughter, dated January 26, 1784

For my own part I wish the Bald Eagle had not been chosen the Representative of our Country. He is a Bird of bad moral Character. He does not get his Living honestly. You may have seen him perched on some dead Tree near the River, where, too lazy to fish for himself, he watches the Labour of the Fishing Hawk; and when that diligent Bird has at length taken a Fish, and is bearing it to his Nest for the Support of his Mate and young Ones, the Bald Eagle pursues him and takes it from him.

With all this Injustice, he is never in good Case but like those among Men who live by Sharping & Robbing he is generally poor and often very lousy. Besides he is a rank Coward: The little King Bird not bigger than a Sparrow attacks him boldly and drives him out of the District. He is therefore by no means a proper Emblem for the brave and honest Cincinnati of America who have driven all the King birds from our Country . . .

I am on this account not displeased that the Figure is not known as a Bald Eagle, but looks more like a Turkey. For the Truth the Turkey is in Comparison a much more respectable Bird, and withal a true original Native of America . . . He is besides, though a little vain & silly, a Bird of Courage, and would not hesitate to attack a Grenadier of the British Guards who should presume to invade his Farm Yard with a red Coat on.

The tawny, an African version of the steppe eagle, is an Aquila more interested in carrion than in large prey, and is often seen in the company of vultures. STU PORTER/SHUTTERSTOCK.COM

Ariel Sharon and George W. Bush both flying bald eagles to bring back human bodies from what is apparently a Palestinian village.

One curious fact stands out amidst all martial imagery of eagles: All the virtues being celebrated and symbolized are traditionally "male," but the sex of the bird that embodies them to the highest degree is invariably female. Apparently those who devise such symbols are as ignorant of eagle biology as those Arab falconers, residents of places where falcons do not breed, who could not believe that their most-valued large falcons were female until they saw them lay eggs. Those connoisseurs of eagles, the Kazakhs, have no such illusions. I once asked an eagler in Mongolia if he ever hunted with males. His somewhat unkind reply was that he didn't hunt mice.

Eagles and Art

The first Asian eagle images that are considered unambiguous evidence of falconry are dated considerably later. The beautiful image of a falconer on a horse, already identified with the still-extant Turkic culture, is from the Kara Too Mountains in the Kochkor Valley south of Lake Issyk-kul in Kyrgyzstan and is dated about AD 600.

The practice of falconry seems to have begun in this area and spread east and west on the Silk Road. Early representations of eagles and falconry in China predate even the Kochkor Valley petroglyph. The "Northern Wei" painting (AD 350–450), on a weathered board, shows two saluki-like dogs—from then until today, the "tazi" will be the typical hunting companion of the eagle—chasing a hare with the aid of an eagle above, while an archer rides behind. This painting more resembles Mongolian folk painting today (which often features eagles) than ones of a classical Chinese style.

The only early "classical" Chinese portrait that may be of an eagle is a drawing from the early Tang dynasty tomb of Prince Zanghui (died AD 684) in the northeastern city of Xian, but, like several Chinese birds identified as eagles, it may instead be a goshawk. It too depicts a tazi hound as the hunter's companion.

Apparently the Chinese rightly identified the use of hunting eagles as a practice of the "barbarians," the Turkic nomads who besieged the empire from west and north of the Great Wall. It is interesting that this identification persists in modern pop culture; in the movie *Crouching Tiger, Hidden Dragon,* the barbarian lover of the female protagonist has a trained eagle that feeds them.

Eagles are therefore scarce in high Eastern art until they reappear in Japan in the 1600s. Amidst many portraits of goshawks, the aristocratic

An early Chinese painting is the first known depiction of an eagle with rider and obvious "tazi" hounds. STEPHEN SELBY

bird of falconry under the shoguns (invariably called "falcons" in museum collections) are images of the *kumataka*, the "bear hawk," or mountain hawk, eagle—both a bird of practical peasant falconry, used to catch fur-bearing animals like fox and raccoon-dog in the northern island of Hokkaido, and an image of power for Japanese artists through the time of Hiroshige.

To the West the depiction of eagles became more symbolic and less realistic. Even such pre-scientific treatises as Emperor Frederic II's *De Arte Venandi cum Avibus,* which attempted to describe birds of prey from observation rather than by citing Aristotle and which anticipated Western knowledge of migration by five hundred years (Frederic lived in Sicily, where he could observe migrant birds as they stacked up in places like the Straits of Messina), depicted birds in a stylized manner. Renaissance painters often painted realistic birds in the margins and backgrounds of their works. But later natural history illustration, until the late eighteenth and early nineteenth centuries, used (badly) stuffed birds as models in stiff poses with lumpy bodies and contorted feet.

In the late nineteenth century there was a fad for finely done but mythical popular portraits of eagles attacking humans. A book called *The Living World,* compiled in 1889 by one J. G. Buell—a magnificent

A lively but impossible depiction shows an eagle lifting an adult human off the ground in the Alps. THE LIVING WORLD, ILLUSTRATED BY J. W. BUEL (PHILADELPHIA, PA, 1889)

collection of information, misinformation, and art from myriad sources—contains a couple of a splendid examples. One shows an engraving of a golden eagle flapping far above an alpine landscape, its talons buried in the breast of a little girl about half its size, and the caption "Eagle of the Alps carrying off Marie Delax." The other, even more incredible, shows an eagle that must be bigger than the extinct *Harpagornis*, also in an alpine setting, holding a child aloft while engaged in a tug of war with an adult who is belaboring it with a club. The man's feet are lifted clear of the ground! I'll deal with the accompanying accounts in "Eagles as Enemies."

The Caribbean-born American artist John James Audubon (1785–1851) energized the painting of birds by refusing to paint from stuffed models. He shot thousands of birds (though now his name is synonymous with conservation) and wired the freshly killed specimens to a wooden frame in dramatic—some would say *too* dramatic—poses. (It has been justly said that the last thing a bird wanted to see, and often the last thing it ever saw, was the approach of John James Audubon.) Despite such criticisms, he transformed bird and wildlife painting by working for the first time with fresh models in hand. The twentieth-century wildlife painter Louis Agassiz Fuertes wrote: " . . . the overpowering virility of Audubon is shown in the snappy, instantaneous attitudes, and dashing motion of his subjects. He made many errors, but he also left a living record that has been of inestimable value to students."[37]

His methods could be strenuous. In the *Ornithological Biography* he describes his preparations for painting the golden eagle:

> I occupied myself a whole day in watching his
> movements; on the next I came to a determination
> as to the position in which I might best represent
> him; and on the third thought of how I could take

---

37 Roger Tory Peterson & Virginia Marie Peterson. *Audubon's Birds of America* (New York, London, and Paris, 1991), unnumbered pages.

away his life with the least pain to him. I consulted several persons on the subject, and among others my most worthy and generous friend, George Parkman, Esq. M.D., who kindly visited my family every day. He spoke of suffocating him by means of burning charcoal, of killing him by electricity, &c. and we both concluded that the first method would probably be the easiest for ourselves, and the least painful to him. Accordingly the bird was removed in his prison into a very small room, and closely covered with blankets, into which was introduced a pan of lighted charcoal, when the windows and doors were fastened, and the blankets tucked beneath the cage. I waited, expecting every moment to hear him fall down from his perch; but after listening for *hours,* I opened the door, raised the blankets, and peeped under them amidst a mass of suffocating fumes. There stood the Eagle on his perch, with his bright unflinching eye turned towards me, as lively and vigorous as ever! . . .

Early next morning I tried the charcoal anew, adding to it a quantity of sulphur, but we were nearly driven from our home in a few hours by the stifling vapours, while the noble bird continued to stand erect, and to look defiance at us whenever we approached his post of martyrdom. His fierce demeanour precluded all internal application, and at least I was compelled to resort to a method always used as the last expedient, and a most effectual one. I thrust a long pointed piece of steel through his heart,

John James Audubon painted this golden eagle for Birds of America.

when my proud prisoner instantly fell dead, without
even ruffling a feather.[38]

Whatever the stress on the eagle and the artist, the result was one
of his most striking and characteristic paintings. The eagle struggles
dramatically to rise, grasping a rabbit in midair; in the background
a figure alleged to be the artist himself makes his way across a log
bridging a chasm between romantic, snowcapped peaks. In his
rucksack rests a big bird—perhaps the golden eagle itself.

Romanticism was in the air. Suddenly eagles were not the mere
mythical monsters of popular art, killing lambs and carrying off
children, nor were their mountainous haunts thought of as ugly places
unfit for habitation. Eagles might still be of "bad character," but they
were also noble, vessels of the sublime. Alfred Lord Tennyson's poetic
fragment *The Eagle*, written in 1851 (the year of Audubon's death)
summarizes the new view, evoking the majesty of both the eagle and
the landscape:

> He clasps the crag with crooked hands;
>   Close to the sun in lonely lands,
> Ringed with the azure world, he stands.
>
> The wrinkled sea beneath him crawls;
>   He watches from his mountain walls,
>   And like a thunderbolt he falls.

Eagles were also illustrated in what was becoming a new genre, the
travelogue of exotic places. In 1858 and 1860 an English artist named
Thomas Witlam Atkinson published two books about his travels and
adventures in Central Asia, *Oriental and Western Siberia*[39] and *Travels*

38 Audubon. *Writings and Drawings*, pp. 355–56.
39 Thomas Witlam Atkinson. *Oriental and Western Siberia* (New York, 1858).

DEFENDING THE BALD EAGLE

**From *Waterton's Wanderings in South America*;
Charles Waterton, Esq., 1885**

By observing the birds in their native haunts, he has been
enabled to purge their history of numberless absurdities,
which inexperienced theorists had introduced into it. It is
a pleasing and a brilliant work. We have no description of
birds in any European publication that can come up to this.
By perusing Wilson's "Ornithology" attentively before I left
England, I knew where to look for the birds, and immediately
recognized them in their native land.

Since his time, I fear the White-headed Eagles have been
much thinned. I was perpetually looking out for them, but saw
very few. One or two came now and then, and soared in lofty
flight over the falls of Niagara. The Americans are proud of this
bird in effigy, and their hearts rejoice when its banner is unfurled.
Could they not then be persuaded to protect the white-headed
eagle and allow it to glide in safety over its own native forests?
Were I an American, I should think I had committed a kind of
sacrilege in killing the white-headed eagle. The Ibis was held
sacred by the Egyptians; the Hollanders protect the Stork; the
Vulture sits unmolested on the top of the houses in the city of
Angustura; and Robin-red-breast, for his charity, is cherished
by the English:

"No burial these pretty babes
    Of any man receives.
Till robin-red-breast painfully
    Did cover them with leaves."

in the Regions of the Upper and Lower Amoor.[40] These gave the first English-language accounts of hunting with golden eagles, which he rendered as "bearcootes" and to which we will return later. As an artist he was also well equipped to illustrate his subjects, and his engravings of berkuts attacking wolves and deer are both accurate in detail and romantically dramatic (with some license; it is unlikely that groups of eagles would willingly attack a pack of wolves!).

Later Victorian and Edwardian artists like Archibald Thorburn and Joseph Wolf were heirs to the romantic tradition. They had great technical skills but could be conventional and sentimental; Wolf in particular painted dramatic scenes with obvious "heroes" and "villains." Thorburn's portraits of dignified, noble eagles could be perfect illustrations for Tennyson's poem.

Impressionism came to nature painting from the north rather than the south. Sweden's Bruno Liljefors (1860–1939), a self-described "painter of animal portraits," was also the best known of the so-called Northern Impressionists and by any standard one of the greatest wildlife painters of all time. He used large canvasses, often-loose brushwork, and situated the animal firmly in its environment. He painted both drama and quiet moments. Some of his paintings portray the violence of predation, and in others you must look hard to see the subject as revealed by a reflection in still water or the glint of an eye.

Eagles, both golden and sea, are among Liljefors's favorite subjects. A theme he returns to again and again is of a sea eagle, or a pair, hunting divers or eiders. The eagles will force the diver to go under repeatedly until it is out of air and then pluck it from the surface. As these boldly patterned seabirds are other favored subjects, the combination must have been irresistible. Another well-known portrait shows a golden eagle about to strike a hare on a hillside, a glint of light like an ember in its eye. It looks "real" to me, though contemporary nature artist Lars Jonsson has some criticisms.

---

40 Thomas Witlam Atkinson. *Travels in the Regions of the Upper and Lower Amoor* (London, 1860).

Archibald Thorburn (1860–1935) painted heroic golden eagles that were perfect examples of the romantic nineteenth-century view of the Scottish highlands. Wikimedia

This eagle attacking a hare is by the Swedish impressionist Bruno Liljefors. TONY ANGELL

Roger Tory Peterson (1908–96) combined science and portraiture to bring birds to the masses with his 1934 *Field Guide to the Birds*. He drew on the work of artist and popular storyteller Ernest Thompson Seton to invent a bold, simplified style that presented a series of related birds on a page, with arrows indicating the identifying "field marks." While his field guides had little effect on fine art, later artists like Liljefors-influenced Lars Jonsson of Sweden would eventually make fine art out of the field guide.[41] Jonsson's gallery work exemplifies a realistic impressionism; he has criticized his greatest influence, Liljefors, for departing from strict naturalism and "heraldization" in his painting of the golden eagle and the hare. And in an example of globalization and today's increased communication, he has recently painted a pair of golden eagles that live near my home in New Mexico,

41 Lars Jonsson. *Birds of Europe* (Princeton, 1993).

A modern "Celtic" eagle belt buckle was made for the author by Scottish artist and engraver Malcolm Appleby. PHOTO FROM THE COLLECTION OF THE AUTHOR.

complete with the mountain peaks I can see outside my window as I type these words. It would be hard to imagine Liljefors in New Mexico.

Another well-known realist-impressionist is California's Thomas Quinn, whose painting style is also heavily influenced by Asian techniques and composition. He is a watercolorist who paints from life; his favorite subjects include birds of prey, especially the golden eagle, waterbirds, and large mammals.

Russia's finest wildlife artist, Vadim Gorbatov, is becoming known worldwide since the end of the Soviet Union. That country froze older traditions in ice, preserving a kind of Romantic realism no longer fashionable elsewhere. Gorbatov, unlike most Western painters, often incorporates humans and their practices into his work. He has traveled among the Kazakhs and other Asian peoples and has done many well-researched depictions of historical and modern falconry.

The Literary Eagle

There were few literary mentions of eagles before the romantics. In America in the late nineteenth century, Walt Whitman wrote of the eagles' courtship, as mentioned in the "Natural History" chapter. In

THE EAGLE IN SCOTLAND

From *Sketches of the Wild Sports & Natural History of the Highlands*; Charles St. John, 1878

How picturesque he looks, and how perfectly he represents the *genius loci* as, perched on some rocky point or withered tree, he sits unconcerned in wind and storm, motionless and statue-like, with his keen, stern eye, however, intently following every movement of the shepherd or the sportsman, who, deceived by his apparent disregard, attempts to creep within rifle-shot. Long before he can reckon on reaching so far with his bullet, the bird launches himself into the air, and gradually sweeping upwards, wheels high out of shot, leaving his enemy disappointed and vexed at having crept in vain through bog and over rock in expectation of carrying home so glorious a trophy of his skill.

the twentieth century a growing interest in nature combined with an increasing unease with industrial society set the scene for a different kind of nature poetry.

Robinson Jeffers (1887–1962) was born in Pennsylvania but moved to California as a young man. He met his wife, Una, in graduate school; she was older and married to a lawyer at the time. They eloped, causing a scandal, and settled on the rugged coast of California. Jeffers began to write his controversial poems, taking as their subject the wild coast and its human and animal inhabitants. He wrote long narrative tragedies in blank verse and many short lyrics. He believed in the tragic evanescent beauty of the physical world and that modern civilization was a temporary and even negative condition. He called his philosophy "inhumanism," which may be summed up by his often-quoted lines:

> ... man dissevered from the earth and stars
>   and his history ... for contemplation or in fact ...
> Often appears atrociously ugly. Integrity is wholeness,
>   The greatest beauty is
> Organic wholeness, the wholeness of life and things, the divine
> beauty
>   Of the universe. Love that, not man
> Apart from that, or else you will share man's pitiful confusions
>   Or drown in despair when his days darken.[42]

Because of such sentiments, and despite his deep personal conservatism, he became an icon to the environmental movement that came into being after his death.

With what he thought of as their pride and stoicism, as well as their beauty, hawks and eagles were important to Jeffers' personal mythology. In his epic *Cawdor*, a caged golden eagle is shot; in a section often excerpted as "The Caged Eagle's Death Dream," he imagines a kind of immortality first, giving the eagle's spirit a perspective that sees birds and cultures rise and fall on the Pacific coast.

> It saw from the height and desert space of
>   Unbreathable air
> Where meteors make green fire and die, the ocean dropping
>   Westward to the girdle of the pearls of dawn
> And the hinder edge of the night sliding toward Asia; it saw
>   Far under eastward the April-delighted

---

42 Robinson Jeffers. *Selected Poems* (New York, 1938), pp. 186–87.

Continent; and time relaxing about it now, abstracted from
being,
      It saw the eagles destroyed,
Mean generations of gulls and crows taking their world: turn
      For turn in the air, as on earth
The white faces drove out the brown. It saw the white
decayed
      And the brown from Asia returning;
It saw men learn to outfly the hawk's brood and forget it
again;
      It saw men cover the earth and again
Devour each other and hide in caverns, be scarce as wolves. It
      Neither wondered nor cared, and it saw
Growth and decay alternate forever, and the tides returning.[43]

Late in life, he made his theories of change and decay and return
even more explicit, comparing what he saw as the unchanging nature
of humans to the beaks of eagles:

The she-eagle is older than I; she was here when the fires of
      Eighty-five raged on these ridges,
She was lately fledged and dared not hunt ahead of them but ate
      Scorched meat. The world has changed in her time;
Humanity has multiplied, but not here; men's hopes and
thoughts
      And customs have changed, their powers are enlarged,
Their powers and their follies have become fantastic,
The unstable animal has never changed so rapidly. The
      Motor and the plane and the great war have gone over
him,

---

43 Robinson Jeffers. *Selected Poems* (New York, 1938), pp. 186–87.

And Lenin has lived and Jehovah died: while the mother-eagle
Hunts her same hills, crying the same beautiful and lonely cry
and
      Is never tired; dreams the same dreams,
And hears at night the rock-slides rattle and thunder in the
throats
      Of these living mountains.
                                  It is good for man
To try all changes, progress and corruption, powers, peace and
      Anguish, not to go down the dinosaur's way
Until all his capacities have been explored; and it is good for
him
To know that his needs and nature are no more changed in fact
      In ten thousand years than the beaks of eagles.

A later twentieth century poet, James Dickey, was more explicit in
his environmentalism. In his poem "The Last Wolverine," he imagines
the beast climbing an arctic tree to mate with the last eagle:

Dear God of the wildness of poetry, let them mate
To the death in the rotten branches,
Let the tree sway and burst into flame
And mingle them, crackling with feathers,

In crownfire. Let something come
Of it something gigantic legendary

Rise beyond reason over hills
Of ice . . . SCREAMING that it cannot die,
That it has come back, this time
On wings, and will spare no earthly thing:

That it will hover, made purely of northern
Lights, at dusk and fall
On men building roads: will perch

On the moose's horn like a falcon
Riding into battle into holy war against
Screaming railroad crews: will pull
Whole traplines like fibres from the snow

In the long-jawed night of fur trappers.

His last haunting line is far from the stony stoicism of Jeffers:

Lord let me die but not die
Out.[44]

Eagles in Popular Culture

I know of no "serious" fiction about eagles, perhaps because the character of animals is not yet considered a serious subject. Popular culture is more accommodating, whether it be thriller novels or the name of a pop band.

In the early 1950s George and Kay Evans, better known for their writing on bird dogs, were writing mystery stories under the pen name "Brandon Bird." In 1954's *Hawk Watch* they invented a splendid example of the Evil Eagle and the Evil Eagler: The bird is introduced in the act of attempting to kill an English setter puppy. Of course it will be trained to go after humans. The protagonist's attitude toward it after it kills the dog couldn't be clearer: "Now all I wanted was to blast it out of the air and tramp its head in." Curiously the more "feminine" female peregrine in the novel is seen as good (the gender of the huge eagle is assumed to be male).

---

44 James Dickey. *Poems 1957–1967* (New York, 1968), pp. 277–78.

Hawk Watch *(1954), a mystery written under a pseudonym by the sporting authors George and Kay Evans, featured a trained eagle as a villain.*

In 1981's *Peregrine*, a genetically enhanced peregrine, is the servant of a ritualistic serial killer, who also desires to train a woman using falconry methods. The great female hunting bird goes up to duel over the skies of Manhattan with the *kumataka*, the hawk eagle, of a Japanese master falconer and kills it.

The recurrent dream of a falcon killing an eagle is a theme in spy novelist's Charles McCarry's 2004 *Old Boys*[45] in which a team

---

45 Charles McCarry. *Old Boys* (Woodstock and New York, 2004), p. 458.

of aging retired CIA agents attempt to find a fanatically religious Arab who possesses "suitcase" nuclear weapons by tracking the migration of the houbara bustard, the great traditional quarry of Arab falconers, across Central Asia. They obtain a precious white saker falcon to tempt the ancient holy man. McCarry's book has a stronger grounding in reality: Arabs do prize sakers, do follow the houbara (Osama bin Laden was alleged to have done so), and there is actually a rarely used method of training falcons to kill eagles, which we will examine in "Eagles as Enemies." McCarry, who has worked in Asia and Africa, was given a trained eagle in Morocco. He gives a vivid description of an aerial battle; his ambivalence about the birds appears to echo his protagonist's mixed admiration and enmity for the desert tribesmen.

> And then, seeming even whiter and swifter than usual in contrast to the bruised hues of the discoloured sky, the Saker falcon was flying. Its great wings propelled it upward in a near vertical climb and soon it was hundreds of feet above the eagles. Then it dove. I had seen this before, of course, but the speed and verticality of the descent took my breath away. It hit one of the eagles. The eagle seemed to explode, dark feathers and blood flying. The eagle shrieked, or I imagined that it did, as the two great birds, striking at each other, tumbling toward earth.

Daniel P. Mannix was an eccentric naturalist and writer and also a falconer. In the late 1930s he and his new wife moved to Taxco in Mexico to make a film about hunting iguanas with eagles: their bald eagle, Aquila, and their golden, Tequila. They were successful in this and other animal endeavors, and subsequently both wrote books about their experiences. Julie's was called *Married to Adventure*

(1954) and featured a cover photo of her on horseback with a hooded bald eagle; Daniel's *All Creatures Great and Small* (1963) showed him with his golden.

In 1978 he put his memories of hunting with eagles to work in *The Wolves of Paris*, a retelling of the historical siege of Paris by a pack of man-killing wolves in the winter of 1439. He imagines a German falconer hiring on to kill the wolves and their "king," the half-dog Cortaud. Interestingly the mercenary has a child who wears a wolf skin to lure back the eagle if she strays—interesting because the German-Finnish eagler Remmler, who will figure in "Eagles as Allies," used a child in a padded wolf hide to train his birds early in the twentieth century.

But the most *noteworthy* popular culture appearance of an eagle may have been in the second-ever made-for-television movie, 1971's *Harpy*.

The covers of Daniel and Julie Mannix's memoirs both show their hunting eagle film stars.

Based on a story by T. K. Brown that appeared in *Playboy* magazine, it embodies many conflicting eagle myths, attitudes, and realities; also of interest are the differences between the story and the film.

Harpy, in both versions, is the story of an architect who is a falconer, his attempts to train a South American harpy eagle, and his conflicts with his ex-wife. The story is a stark version, almost Ayn-Randian if not Nietzschean. The bird is a symbol of power and freedom, and the falconer achieves freedom by dominating the bird. Again there is a falcon-eagle conflict; the architect sacrifices his peregrine to the eagle to see whether the eagle is strong enough to overcome it (something that would never happen in the real world, by the way). His assistant, the young Native American, John, objects:

> "It's a shame, boss," John said. "You shouldn't do it. They're both fine birds."
>
> "I have to know about the eagle," Robin said. "I have to know how much she has in her."
>
> "She's not built to fight falcons," the Indian said, "and no natural falcon would ever go after her. It's a waste and a shame."
>
> "I have to know what that eagle has in her," Robin repeated with great vigor. "Don't you understand? If she wins against the falcon she is the mightiest creature in the world."
>
> "And you are its master," Marian said. "Is that it?"
>
> "Yes," he said. "I guess that's it."[46]

In both versions, despite the sanity of her observation above, Marian is a near-psychotic obsessive ex-wife whose dependency threatens the architect's (called for no obvious reason "Peter" in the film) carefully constructed life. But in the story what she threatens

---

46 Hugh M. Hefner, ed. *The Playboy Reader* (Chicago, 1968), p. 111.

above all is his freedom. He decides to kill her with the eagle after she kills his other birds, though in a last bout of sentimentality he calls Marian to turn her face so that the "dreadful talons" do not "mar the beautiful once-beloved face."

The movie is less cruel in its sentimentality. The story is opened up, and the architect is given a fiancée (his secretary) for the ex-wife to abuse as well. She also sets up the young Indian for a rape charge before she kills Peter's other birds with his knife.

From the beginning, the architect, played by former Western star Hugh O'Brian, is made out to be a noble green environmentalist; in one of the first scenes, we see him attempting to sell the design for an environmentally sustainable new town to a boorish, skeptical developer. His falconry is less about power than about achieving his bond with nature. Elizabeth Ashley plays his ex-wife as a selfish heiress and a shrew—or a harpy—who lies to his fiancée and attempts to get the young assistant, on probation for a juvenile crime, to sleep with him and then put in jail. After Marian kills the other birds, it is not the architect but the Indian who engineers her destruction by eagle as she leaves the ranch in an open convertible (he has trained the eagle by using a mop—apparently it is supposed to resemble human hair—as a lure).

Even the harpy, one of the great jungle eagles, seems benign, with large dark eyes and a sweet chirp, and barely shows any aggression even when she "kills"—special effects were not advanced in 1971—a wild wolf (in the hills above Santa Monica!). In her final scene she perches serenely above the burning wreck of Marian's convertible, a figure of sympathy whose only "crime" was that she has killed a despicable character.

The falconry, unlike that in the print version, is well done and realistically portrayed. The actors carry, handle, and fly their avian partners in a way that indicates to a knowing eye that they too had been trained well, including lessons in handling a bird that would give many falconers pause. Although it has never been released as a DVD, it has a cult reputation among America's falconers, and there is a lively traffic in bootleg copies.

Allegedly the naturalist and filmmaker Jim Fowler once wrecked his car and came to his senses upside down in the roof, with his harpy perched on his belly. It is tempting to wonder if the movie's last scene is a tribute to this legend; very few harpies have ever been flown in America.

The only other eagle film in English is a documentary called *Kyran over Mongolia*. It is at a far higher level of art than *Harpy*, but its subject properly belongs to the next chapter.

CHAPTER 3

EAGLES AS ALLIES: FALCONRY

"No living man can, or possibly ever will, understand the instinct of predation that we share with our raptorial servant."

—Aldo Leopold

Well, maybe not *servant*, exactly.

Shortly before his death the American firearms and shooting writer Col. Jeff Cooper challenged his readers to describe what he called "great classic hunts." I responded, suggesting the Kazakh hunt wolves with golden eagles. He reacted with indignant disbelief: "Puppies, perhaps. Hundred-pounders, unlikely."

But of course Kazakhs do hunt wolves—and foxes, and deer, and antelope—with eagles.

Falconry is defined by dictionaries and on the website of the North American Falconer's Association as "the taking of wild quarry in its natural state and habitat by means of a trained raptor." But as Helen Macdonald says in *Falcon*, "this singularly fails to capture the social, emotional, and historical allure of an activity that has fascinated humans for thousands of years and has taken a most extraordinary variety of forms." She quotes an American falconer who calls it a "virus," a disease, but this is not just a Western conceit; an elderly Kazakh in western Mongolia once told me he didn't want to teach falconry to his grandson because it was an addiction "worse than vodka."

Addiction or sport, falconry must have had practical roots, for it is far too time- (and energy-) consuming to take hold among people struggling to make a living if it brought no rewards but a surge of adrenalin. Our species may be naturally "biophilic," but it is not insane. Roger Tory Peterson once wrote that man emerged from the mists of history with a peregrine perched on his fist, but it might make more sense, at least in terms of falconry, to say he rode out of Central Asia on a shaggy horse with a golden eagle on his arm. Peregrines are elegant fun for a civilization with time on its hands, but eagles are—almost— practical. They can help slay large animals to eat and fur-bearers for their skins and kills wolves for both fur and flock protection.

If you trace falconry in art and history, it seems to spread from a center somewhere in the mountains of Central Asia, whence the Mongols and Turks also came, and moved east and west with the caravans and mounted warriors. Near its roots it uses the practical birds—eagle, goshawk, and saker falcon—and simple tools. As it travels it acquires complications, such as the Japanese lacquered food box and ornate hoods in the West, and begins to use more whimsical birds: the specialized peregrine, the tiny merlin. But the Kazakhs, whose ancestors may have been the first falconers, stuck (and still stick) with the eagles whose images are chiselled into their rocks.

The earliest Western mention of eagle falconry is in that fabulous concoction of reportage and tall tales called *The Travels of Marco Polo,* written (or rather, dictated) in 1298. He wrote at length of the hunting and hawking parties of the Great Khan of China, of trained falcons and lynxes and "leopards" (probably cheetahs). He claimed that the khan employed ten thousand falconers to fly his gyrfalcons,

*This Kazakh hunter, "team," and quarry are by Vadim Gorbatov,
Russia's premiere wildlife artist.* VADIM GORBATOV

peregrines, and sakers, which he followed on a pavilion carried by four
elephants. He was already familiar with the eagles' ultimate quarry:
"His majesty has eagles also, which are trained to stoop at wolves,
and such is their size and strength that none, however large, can escape
from their talons."[47]

The first English-speaking traveler to write about hunting with
eagles seems to have been the artist Thomas Witlam Atkinson, who
wandered Central Asia in the 1850s. He both sketched golden eagles,
which he rendered as "bearcootes," and saw them hunted. From
Oriental and Western Siberia:

> A well-mounted Kirghis held his bearcoote, chained
> to a perch, which was secured into a socket on his

---

47 Marco Polo. *The Travels of Marco Polo* (London, Melbourne, and Toronto, 1983), pp.
   95–100.

saddle. The eagle had shackles and a hood, and was perfectly quiet: he was under the charge of two men. Near to the sultan were his three hunters, or guards, with their rifles, and around us were a band of about twenty Kirghis, in their bright-colored kalats: more than half the number were armed with battle-axes. Taking us altogether, we were a wild-looking group, whom most people would rather behold at a distance than come in contact with . . .

We had not gone far when several large deer rushed past a jutting point of the reeds, and bounded over the plain about three hundred yards from us. In an instant the bearcoote was unhooded and his shackles removed, when he sprang from his perch and soared up into the air. I watched him ascend as he wheeled around, and was under the impression that he had not seen the animals; but in this I was mistaken. He had now risen to a considerable height and seemed to position himself for about a minute. After this he gave two or three flaps with his wings, and swooped off in a straight line toward his prey. I could not perceive that his wings moved, but he went at a fearful speed. There was a shout, and away went his keepers at full gallop, followed by many others. I gave my horse his head and a touch of the whip; in a few minutes he carried me to the front, and I was riding neck-and-neck with one of the keepers. When we were about two hundred yards off the bearcoote struck his prey. The deer gave a bound forward and fell. The bearcoote had struck one talon into his neck, the other into his back, and with his beak was tearing out the animal's liver. The Kirghis sprung from his horse, slipped the hood over the eagle's head and the

Atkinson's bearcoote in action is a bit dramatic. ORIENTAL AND WESTERN SIBERIA BY THOMAS WITLAM ATKINSON

shackles upon his legs, and he was ready for another flight. No dogs are taken out when hunting with the eagle; they would be destroyed to a certainty; indeed, the Kirghis assert that he will attack and kill the wolf. Foxes are hunted in this way, and many are killed; the wild goat and the lesser kinds of deer are also taken in considerable numbers.[48]

Most of his account is in accord with later chronicles, and it is how falconry is practiced in Central Asia today, except for his mention of hunting without dogs. In Kazakhstan today eagles are flown with tazi

---

48 Atkinson. *Oriental and Western Siberia*, pp. 417–18.

hounds, and if wolves are the quarry, a "tobet," or flock protection dog, itself competent to take on wolves, may be added to the mix. But his account of eagles hunting wolves in *The Upper and Lower Amoor* seems a bit . . . imaginative. Also notice that he spells "bearcoote" differently:

> . . . a singular spectacle was presented to our view. A large maral [deer] had been hunted down by three wolves, who had just sensed him, and the ravenous beasts were tearing the noble animal apart while yet breathing. We urgently prepared to inflict punishment on two of the beasts, and crept quietly along under cover to get within range. We succeeded, and were levelling our rifles, when Sergae called my attention to two large bearcoots, passing aloft and preparing for a swoop. He whispered "don't fire, and we shall see some grand sport."
>
> Presently one of the eagles shot down like an arrow, and was almost instantly followed by the other. When within about forty yards of the group, the wolves caught sight of them, and instantly stood on the defensive, showing their long yellow fangs, and uttering a savage howl. In a few seconds the first bearcoot struck his prey; one talon was fixed on his back, the other on the upper part of the neck, completely securing the head, while he tore out the wolf's liver with his beak. The other bearcoot had seized another wolf, and shortly both were as lifeless as the animal they had hunted.[49]

Most now think that eagles do not *naturally* hunt wolves. But in fairness to Atkinson, generally a good observer, Idaho naturalist and

---

49 Atkinson. *Travels in the Regions of the Upper and Lower Amoor*, p. 148.

falconer Charles Browning once flushed one off the still warm carcass of a full-grown coyote.

The next wave of travelers tended to be scientific, scholarly, and sometimes military or diplomatic, and they gave less-romantic descriptions (though it is impossible to entirely eliminate the romance of training a dragonlike flying creature that can kill wolves). Eagles appear in virtually all contemporary books about Central Asia, in the memoirs of diplomats such as C. P. Skrine and Eric Shipton, and in the journals of explorer-scientists such as Douglas Carruthers.

Carruthers is typical. In *Beyond the Caspian*, published in 1949 but mostly dealing with scientific expeditions made before World War I,

A postcard from the 1920s shows a Kyrgiz hunter with his eagle and yurt. STEPHEN BODIO

Gorbatov titled his painting of a flight at a wolf, "Riski Attack."
VADIM GORBATOV

he writes with a dry dispassion, which makes his descriptions of large prey all the more believable:

> . . . the quarry consists mostly of foxes, gazelle, wolves, and, in earlier days, the Saiga antelope. It is said that a good eagle can kill a wolf unaided, but I have never seen it happen. Some authorities, Levchine for instance, declare that a wolf is too strong, and goes off with the eagle still hanging on to it, the eagle is able to hold it with one foot and anchor itself with the other, until the wolf exhausts itself in the struggle! Believe it or not, but one must remember that *smaller* birds of prey, such as Peregrines and Sakers, are habitually flown at gazelle in other countries. These Tian Shan wolves may be a trifle smaller than the Siberian or Tundra wolf, but the difference would scarcely be discernable to any but an expert eye.
>
> Occasionally larger game, such as deer—hinds and calves for choice—form the quarry, but this can

only happen when the deer inhabit suitable country, such as river-jungles on the plains, and not forests in the mountains. Generally speaking, however, larger game is not flown at, unless it is in conjunction with men and dogs, and then the eagle may be used to advantage. In these cases, however, it is not employed to kill, but to fluster the quarry, and so to bring it to bay and bag. Even as the Badawin are in the habit of flying their Saker falcons, succoured by greyhounds, to take ibex and gazelle . . . In this case, obviously, the eagle has little more than a nuisance value, but it is sufficient to fluster the quarry to the extent of putting him at the mercy of unmounted and poorly-armed men.[50]

The American scholar-adventurer Owen Lattimore, later to fall victim (with virtually no evidence) to Senator Joseph McCarthy's smears, was born in the United States but went to China when he was one year old and did not leave for the first time until he was twenty-nine. Raised there, familiar with all the languages, he was also a hunter with a gun and "Chinese greyhound" (Saluki-tazi) and brought an insider's perspective lacking in some of the colonial accounts. In *High Tartary* (1930) he writes of eagles with authority, and of their work with hounds.

Like the hound the *berkut*, the great hunting eagle of the Qazaqs, is used above all for taking foxes. The eagles are captured from the nest, in itself something of an exploit for bold young men, the nest-robber being most often swung out on a rope over bad crags and sometimes attacked by the parent eagles. The

---

50 Douglas Carruthers. *Beyond the Caspian* (London, 1949), pp. 106–7.

eaglet is kept hooded almost from the beginning, and fed choice meat from the hand. It is usually so well in hand by the beginning of its first season that it will return readily to a lure. It is first flown in the autumn of the year after its capture, being then more than a year old. The female, larger than the male, is always the better.

Both hawks and eagles are fasted before being cast at quarry, hawks for seven or eight days and eagles for as much as twenty. When well fasted, they will strike at the first quarry sighted; otherwise they are likely to tower, waiting for quarry of their own choice. A good eagle, when striking at a fox, will fix its talons at the back of the neck, the talons penetrating through the soft base of the skull into the brain and killing it instantly without a flurry or damage to the pelt.

Hounds and eagles are sometimes worked together, to make sure of the quarry, which in doubling back to escape the strike of the bird falls to the hounds. The Qazaqs, however, everywhere maintain that the best of eagles will take even a wolf unaided. All of them assert also that in the eagles' eyries are found the bones and horns of full-grown roe deer (which can weigh forty pounds) and the bones of full-grown wolves. The eagles pass their prime at about seven years. After that they are still good to be flown at hares but no longer at foxes. It is only natural to assume, however, that eagles in the wild state retain their vigor much longer. Among the Qazaqs a good eagle is a possession of much honor; it has a nominal price of two or three good horses, but in fact is rarely bought and sold. It is reserved as a present of more than unusual splendor to tribal chieftains, or exchanged between close friends.[51]

By the 1930s another breed of Western travelers, including women, was beginning to invade the distant roadless places of the world. (To be fair, Atkinson's wife wrote a spirited book in 1863 to clarify the details of daily experiences behind her husband's two volumes, but she wrote it as "Mrs. Atkinson"!) These new travelers, female or male, were looking for exotic experience and often paid their way by writing about their adventures in popular journals and eventually in books. "Travel writing" as a genre had begun. Famous early twentieth-century practitioners included Dame Freya Stark and Peter Fleming, but one of the best—perhaps unfairly eclipsed by her one-time trip companion, Fleming—was the solitary Swiss writer Ella "Kini" Maillart. Her description of a hunting eagle in *Turkestan Solo*, about a trek from the Tian Shan range to the Kizil Kum deserts, is more color than science, vivid and immediate:

> Suddenly rounding a bend, we meet the most impressive sight of all: three Kirghiz riders with eagles on their fists.
> The first is wearing large, dark snow spectacles. The others gaze at us and at our mute astonishment. The birds of prey are enormous; it is the only possible word for them, so mighty that I cannot imagine what other bird could better deserve the title "king of birds."
> From the jutting shoulder the wings hang, their dark, shining plumes like an armour of overlapping plates. The heads of the birds are covered with leather hoods through which they cannot see. The cries they

---

51 Owen Lattimore. *High Tartary* (New York, Tokyo, London, 1994). pp 106–7.

utter sound as though ten doors were screeching on their hinges. The hooked beak is on a level with the man's forehead. The black talons are enormous, and issue from a grey, scaly sheath of skin to grasp the leather glove which, in order that the reins may be held, is cut for only one finger and a thumb. The bird tries to tear a piece off with its beak. A slip-knot fastens a long thong to one foot. The man's fist rests on a wooden fork socketed in the saddle.

The nape of the eagle's neck is a tuft of white disordered feathers. The hood removed, the implacable eye appears, glittering like a jewel.

From the cruppers of a pack-horse, the stiffened skins of wolves, ibex, and marmots hang in quantities.

We sight a marmot, and track it down. The bird, released from its noose, is cast off after it. It does not rise very high, then it swoops down toward the marmot, and cuts off its retreat by settling in front of the warren. The marmot, disturbed by the noise, seeks its hole for refuge, and falls into the fatal talons. The Kirghiz comes up, finishes it off, ties up the eagle again, and give it the entrails to eat.

The marmot will end up in our soup, and Capa stakes a claim to the skin.

"It is the beginning of my fur coat," she says, as she fastens it to her saddle.[52]

One last Western traveler, who did not write about his experiences until much later, must be mentioned here. Dr. Friedrich Wilhelm Remmler, an ethnic German born in Finland in 1888, had an uncle

---

52 Ella Maillart. *Turkestan Solo* (London and Toronto, 1938), p. 116.

who ran Alfred Nobel's oilfields out of Baku on the Caspian and was involved in oil drilling on the "Kirghiz Steppe," now Kazakhstan. (Kazakh and Kirghiz were barely distinguished from each other until Stalin split the Central Asian republics.) The young eagler-to-be, already a passionate hunter, journeyed there in his teens and was inspired to train his own eagles. His methods were eclectic and owed much to his own innovations and the wooded terrain of his native Finland, but he was the first modern Western-style eagler to have intellectual "descendants," as we will see.

Berkutchis remain among the favorite subjects of Russian artist Vadim Gorbatov. Vadim Gorbatov

EAGLE VERSUS FALCON

From *D'Arcussia's Falconry*, 1643; translated by John Loft, 2003

From time to time Eagles kill trained hawks. In this country of Provence we are particularly subject to their attacks, Goshawks most often being the victims, they having no better tactic than to take cover in a tree. From Lyon to Flanders, Eagles are never seen, and some people, not knowing what they are, cannot believe that they are as big as we say or that they can attain the speed of a Falcon. However, they can rest assured that although the Eagle is huge its size does not prevent it from being the swiftest, the strongest, the most dashing, and the most courageous of all birds—qualities that caused the ancients to call it their King, comparing it with the one who has the power to bestow life or death as it may seem good to him. That being so, he must still maintain his high pitch because if he sinks lower he will be forced to give way to hawks inferior to him if they once get above him.

Without the eagles we would keep our hawks longer. For me, I have to pay rent to them twice a year, but not at the same time, as happened to one of my neighbors who has flying two Lanners together. While they were pluming a partridge that they had taken, there came an Eagle, sweeping down and carrying off both Lanners and the partridge, all together. I leave you to imagine how furious he must have been. I do everything I can to exterminate the whole race, for such creatures do harm to every kind of game. All the methods of taking them would make a long list. It can be done with a fowl or a dead dog; they can be killed in the eyrie when they are small; and there are many other ways.

There are seven species of Eagle. The two bad ones are the black, called Royal Eagle, and the red-brown, called Ellion. It was the black of which Horace said that Jupiter had given it power over all other birds and that several nations believed it served as an omen of Imperial grandeur.

I find it very much to the purpose to keep our hawks' jesses very short, since whenever the eagles see them they take them to be the remains of prey and set out to chase and rob them. When that happens you will see that the eagle goes for the jesses first. If having the jesses too short feels awkward, they can be held back with the second and third fingers.

Never spare the wine for those who catch eagles and bring them to you. For my part, I give them a half-écu for every head they deliver, and at that price hope to rid the country of them, for the wrongs they inflict on our hawks. I disregard the many great virtues the ancients once attributed to them, and the honour that many Emperors bestowed on them, in life and death, as many authors have described for us. There is even an incident in the story of Mahomet, who captured Constantinople, how, during a day's flying, two hawks set about an eagle, and, in fact, after a long time spent in striking it and forcing it lower, they drove it to the ground with the strength of their blows. The Falconers were overjoyed, recommending the hawks, which were Sakers, to the King for their daring and courage, and expected to please him. Mahomet commanded them to be killed, and had them beheaded, in order to give a lesson to his entourage by this example.

Asian Eagles Today

Without a doubt I am, at least in today's journalistic niche ecosystem, classifiable as a "travel writer" and a "nature writer." As to the first, I have a (invincibly romantic) deep passion for going places off the mainstream tourist tracks, where there is no fast food and few people speak English. As for the second, I was trained as a biologist, not as a journalist, and have a particular fascination with the flexible boundaries where humans meet nature, whether the subject is domestication, hunting, or conservation. These mixed interests have both entangled me with the lives of animals and set the agenda for my travels. My passions have taken me to places as "civilized" as Provence (in search of the nineteenth-century peasant autodidact Jean-Henri Fabre, pioneer of insect behavior and inspiration to Darwin) and Oxford (to meet the evolutionist-artist Jonathan Kingdon); to Zimbabwe (to study local conservation projects, which led to a case of malaria and a fascination with parasite evolution); and to Central Asia, where I sought out primitive dogs in Kazakhstan and eagles among the Kazakhs of Mongolia. I first went to Mongolia in 1998 with a magazine assignment in my pocket. But I did not go as a journalist, whatever funds and legitimacy the assignment might have given me; I went as a falconer. I have been flying raptors for almost fifty years.

Eagle falconry provokes a peculiar ambivalence in the West, especially in English-speaking countries. The magnificent-but-evil paradigm never quite subsides. Eagles are alleged to be dangerous, "barbaric," and some of this opprobrium rubs off on its practitioners. Prominent "establishment" falconers mutter that restrictions should be put on the use of eagles because a rogue eagle might injure a dog or even a child; in such circles even wanting to own an eagle is a sign of bad character. As though justifying these beliefs, eagles are alleged to be, at least in captivity, "bad" or lazy hunters. People who have never been to Asia or even seen a video will tell you that Kazakhs and

Kirghiz starve their birds, that these birds are so weak that they can only fly downhill at hares, that all films about them are done with "bagged" or tethered quarry.

A few people dissented. Wyoming's Dan McCarron, a seasoned hunter, predator caller, and eagler who met and learned from Remmler when he was a child near Niagara Falls and inherited his equipment, doubted the conventional take. "We need to talk to the grandfathers!" he would exclaim. "How do they check their weight? How do they know how much to feed them? How do they moult them? *What is the historical truth?*"

I was inclined to Danny's point of view, if only because the accounts I have quoted above seemed to portray active, self-willed, independent hunters that could be trusted with dogs. The fall of the Soviet Union (which like China today disapproved of both the distraction from economic pursuits and the tribal symbolism of hunting with birds) and the first stirrings of ecotourism in the Altai and the Tian Shan led to my contacting an English-speaking Kazakh entrepreneur in the far-western Mongolian state of Bayaan Olgii. Canat was eager to set up a business taking rugged Western trekkers to the deserts and mountains of Mongolia, and an obsessed falconer willing to go there in February without a group seemed to provide a good test case. (Eagles are flown mostly in winter, as their quarries' pelts are at their prime then and stock animals like sheep, which require tending, are not born until late February.)

The books, not the naysayers, were right of course. Kazakh falconers had a practical and intuitive grasp of eagle behavior that made training them look easy. They had techniques for raising birds from babies and for trapping and training young adults. Some eaglers preferred the almost-melodious and fairly continuous yelping of trained youngsters because, as they do not use the leg bells of traditional Western falconry, it was easier to find the birds when they were out of sight. Others liked the older birds, "passagers" in the

Western parlance, because they knew more about hunting and, once they were tamed, had better manners (although these were harder to train to catch wolves).

The first eagler I met, the late R. Sulieman of Bayaan Nuur village, was a "grandfather," a short and merry man with two eagles, both started young. He showed me how to feel his eagles' thighs, ventral bones, and breast keel for fat and muscle (unlike Westerners, Asian falconers use no scales to measure weights), all the time reassuring me that "of course you know this already" (I didn't). His birds were calm and showed no aggression whatsoever on being handled by a

The late R. Suleiman points to a cliff he intends to hunt from.
STEPHEN BODIO

stranger, even when he flew both to the same lure made from a hare skin and a fox tail sewed together and garnished with marmot meat. Although they both buried their feet in the lure, they fed calmly, each alternately bowing to gobble a mouthful then raising her head to look around. Despite my wariness—their spread, "mantling" wings could be read as a sign of aggression—he encouraged me to move in with my camera until I was just a foot away, lying on my belly at their feet. He then took my right hand and extended it to the nearest eagle's leg. She raised her head, looked me in the eye, and lowered her head to eat another mouthful.

Manai's winter house and two pelts of animals killed by his eagles: a fox and a wolf. Stephen Bodio

A few years later and a few miles to the southwest, I was enjoying a cup of buttered "milk tea" with Canat's cousin Manai, an eagler who specializes in passage—wild-caught young adults—with whom I had hunted on the previous trip. Through Canat, he told us that his eleven-year-old son had seen a wolf a few days before in the Altai foothills behind his log and mud "winter-spending place." When we saw his son riding in through the swirling snow, my wife, Libby, went out to see her first Kazakh bird. The boy nodded, dismounted, flopped the hooded bird to the ground, and removed her hood. He took Libby's hand and stroked the eagle's bare head with it as though the immense bird was a spaniel and then picked her up and rehooded her. When they came inside, Canat told us they had flown at a small wolf but missed it. I should add that there was a fresh *large* wolf pelt hanging from the exposed roof beam outside.

In my entire time in the Kazakh country, through three trips to two countries over several years, I have seen one aggressive eagle, and she was owned by the rather sour old man who considered falconry to be like an addiction. Not that there are not aggressive eagles: One had allegedly killed a child (and had its feet cut off in revenge) a few years before; another, less deadly but surely overly ambitious, had attacked a snow leopard, which killed her. But the general standard was that eagles were tame and calm, and expected to be that way. Not only did they not eat the children, the children took them out to hunt wolves!

The other slander on eagles, still repeated at least in some US circles (by falconers who believe that they can do better, although they have not) is the canard that they are weak, starved, flown only downhill at tied rabbits, etc., ad nauseam. The early accounts already point to such interpretations as utter nonsense, delusions of Western superiority in all things compounded with wishful thinking. (Interestingly, such overly hungry eagles would tend to be aggressive rather than calm and friendly, seeing everything as possible prey or a rival.) I can testify personally that I never encountered an eagle with the concave-sided,

Two young hunters administer sweet hot tea to the berkut to give her energy. STEPHEN BODIO

Looking out over the steppe for quarry near Bayan Nuur, Olgii, Mongolia. STEPHEN BODIO

hollow-ground chest keel of a starving raptor—all were rounded and well muscled. More importantly they flew well, even in high winds. I only saw one kill, on a fox, but the flight was spectacular. Manai's big wolf-hunting female left his fist as he sat on his horse on a knife-back ridge. She soared up, climbed into the wind until she was fifty or sixty meters above him, then turned back downwind and fell like a hammer on the fox that was zigzagging through the ledges below Manai. It was a performance by an athlete at the top of her ability.

Finally, Central Asian falconry is utterly practical (although I will let Manai add that "it is the most interesting thing I know"). I was amused by a photographer on one of my assignments who kept trying to get shots that excluded trucks, baseball caps, and the ubiquitous Russian motorcycles with sidecars that vie with horse and camel as

Tazi breeder Wolfgang Regar photographed another version of the team near Nura, Kazakhstan, a town of berkutchis. W. REGAR, SWITZERLAND

the most common mode of transportation in remote Asian locations. My thought was that if it had been, say, 1700, the scenes we saw would not have been remarkable. But after a century and a half of Russian occupation and sometimes repression, plus the coming of Western technology—from the automobile to the Internet (an English-speaking Kazakh told me that he had "no indoor toilet, but Internet in my house")—eagles were still used as traditional hunting partners. Incorporation of modern technology when it is useful seems a sign that eagle culture is healthy and evolving rather than merely a stagnant, idealized cultural symbol.

I was amused by a photographer on one of my assignments who kept trying to get shots that excluded trucks, baseball caps, and the ubiquitous Russian motorcycles with sidecars that vie with horse and camel as the most common mode of transportation in remote Asian locations. My thought was that if it had been, say, 1700, the scenes we saw would not have been remarkable.

The first eagle I saw in Mongolia, one of Sulieman's, used a tractor tire for a perch. Her jesses or leg bands—I brought back a pair—were made of some kind of synthetic material bonded to wool on the inside, to protect her leg feathers, though the long straps that dangled behind were made of braided horse hide and ended in medieval-style brass rings, or "varvels."

In Kazakhstan eagles are now sometimes taken out to hunt in motorcycle sidecars rather than on horseback. (Such machines go everywhere, even on roads too rough for ordinary cars.) Recently some Kazakh falconers there sent me a series of slightly foggy photos

The plume of an eagle owl or "ukhu" is attached to a berkut's wing to give her more spiritual power. STEPHEN BODIO

Wolfgang Regar photographed hunting from a sidecar out of Nura.
W. Regar, Switzerland

indicating that the oldest falconry in the world may be getting feedback from some of the newest. In the past twenty years, innovative falconers in the United States and Africa have learned to fly Harris's hawks (United States) and African hawk eagles (Zimbabwe) at hares at night with the aid of spotlights. The Kazakh photos show an eagler perched atop a Russian UAZ four-wheel-drive vehicle in the dark, a fox in a spotlight, and a blurry collision, followed by a clear photo of an eagle with a red fox. I can't help but be tickled by the postmodern, international feedback loops in this most ancient of sports.

The author hunted with these three riders in far western Mongolia.
STEPHEN BODIO

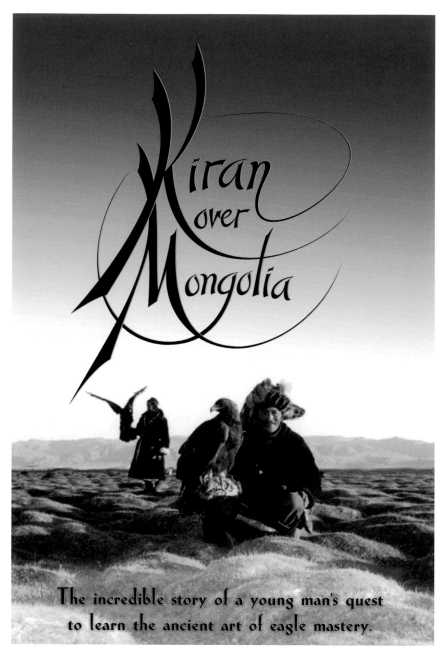

The incredible story of a young man's quest
to learn the ancient art of eagle mastery.

"'Kyran Over Mongolia' is a brilliant documentary film about
becoming a berkutchi in Mongolia. JOSEPH SPAID

Recently New York documentary filmmaker Joseph Spaid traveled to western Mongolia to film the education of a young eagle hunter. The result, *Kyran over Mongolia,* is now in limited release. "Kyran," the Kazakh word for "golden," is also used for both the birds themselves and for an indefinable condition akin to nobility possessed by the best birds and falconers. The documentary is a brilliant and unflinching record of all eagle training, from trapping the bird to her taking her first fox.

Unusual Eagle Falconry

Three other eagle practices, one very old and two extremely new, deserve mention before we again pick up the tail of contemporary Western eaglery.

The old one, seeming to follow directly in the line of practical Asian eagle and goshawk falconry, is the use of the bear-hawk, or *kumataka,* known in the West as the mountain hawk eagle *(Spizaetus nipalensis).* Japanese falconry has developed a few odd local practices. A wooden food box with a sliding lid is used to call in the bird, rather than a lure in the shape of an animal, and most training starts with extremely severe dieting. But in Japan, especially in the northern island of Hokkaido, the *kumataka* is used to take such useful (for fur) quarry as fox and raccoon dog in straightaway downhill pursuit rather than for "art."

Dr. E. W. Jameson describes some techniques in *The Hawking of Japan:*

> The first introduction to quarry is done through a
> stuffed hare skin, a rough imitation of the hawk's
> intended prey. The hawk should be placed on a perch
> some sixty feet away. The falconer produces the hare
> skin, dragging it along the ground in clear view of
> the waiting bird. When the hawk flies to the skin, she
> should be rewarded with a piece of meat from the
> food box; this is done several times each day, each

time from a greater distance. When the bird dives at the skin with genuine spirit and gusto, the lure may be replaced by a live hare.

The hawk eagle then progresses to "real" prey:

> The manner of clutching the quarry is important, especially in the case of formidable enemies such as foxes and raccoon-dogs. The method of holding hares varies among individual birds: some will grab the head and others will bind to the loin. When attacking dangerous game such as badgers, raccoon-dogs, and foxes, the kumataka must be both cautious and bold, and for these creatures the hawk has a special technique. From above and behind, the bird grabs the prey by the hindquarters and back with both feet, and as soon as the prey turns its head, the bird clutches the jaws with one foot. The hawk then holds the enemy powerless. The skill and effectiveness of this method are magnificent beyond description. If the hawk fails in its first attempt to seal the muzzle of the fox, he will then hold the fox's head with both feet, in which case it will have difficulty in preventing the mammal's jumping about. If the bird cannot grip both the head and loins of the fox, he will have great difficulty in killing the prey by himself. The bird may sometimes be killed unless the two combatants become separated. The hawk well understands the danger of its quarry and also knows its vulnerable points, but, nevertheless, the moment of the dive is a tense and anxious one for the falconer.[53]

---

53 Dr. E. W. Jameson. *The Hawking of Japan*, p. 60.

The Kazakhs seem less worried about children and eagles than the Japanese. STEPHEN BODIO

Although the *kumataka* is considerably smaller than the golden eagle, Japanese falconers seem to consider it to be a dangerous bird, more than the Kazakhs do their berkuts. Jameson writes: "Great care must be given to see that children do not go near the hawk house when birds are there for these birds are very fast and deadly. Also, kumataka will attack domestic dogs and cats if the falconer is not careful to prevent their coming next to the hawk house."

Despite the practical nature of the hunt with the *kumataka*, Japanese artists have long painted lovely images of the species. In 1967 a Japanese photographer took a series of black-and-white photos of a winter hunt that resemble classical Japanese ink-brush painting. They were published that year in *Sports Illustrated* and published in 1969 in *Life* magazine.

In Zimbabwe, or rather in Rhodesia before it was Zimbabwe, several white soldiers in the civil war that preceded the country's emergence saw great numbers of springhares on their night patrols. As several were falconers, they began taking their African hawk eagles out to fly at the hares under the spotlights of their armored vehicles—a story that would be nearly unbelievable if not for the photos!

Perhaps the most physically dangerous eagle used in modern falconry is a crowned eagle *(Stephanoaetus coronatus)* that was trained, also in Zimbabwe, in the 1990s. Andre Gruenwald used her for "control" against monkey damage on plantations. According to an article by Craig Golden in the December 1997 issue of *American*

"Old 'Berkut' Last Light," is the author's favorite painting by Russian artist Vadim Gorbatov. "It reminds me," the author said, "of several old hunters now gone." VADIM GORBATOV

Falconer, the bird was started on relatively easy quarry like hares (at night), graduating to small antelope in her second year and to the powerful, intelligent monkeys (which are social and fight back) in her third. Although she was not particularly large as eagles go, flying in the high-seven-, low-eight-pound range, she sounded intimidating: Gruenwald is quoted as saying of her training that:

> The first few scrub hares she caught, I allowed her
> to feed on at the site (taking about an hour), but this
> was short lived as she would fly at me with much
> meaning, hit the glove, then go straight back to her
> kill and mantle.
>
> This was extremely dangerous, and so I trained
> her to release the quarry and feed on the glove as to
> gain control once she was on the glove. She would
> then be fed on her kill once properly secured on her
> perch in the mew. The mew [hawk house] would then
> not be entered into for two days . . . she would even
> protect the remaining bones . . .
>
> Handling Lundi is like handling a loaded
> shotgun—she could put numerous holes in you in
> seconds and the threat of something more serious
> was always there.[54]

Perhaps. But unlike a shotgun, "Lundi" has volition; crowned eagles are dedicated primate hawks in nature and have been implicated in several attacks on humans (see next chapter). Although she eventually became a reliable hunter, Golden confessed to me that he didn't like to see her looking at him before she had been allowed to hunt and take her "edge" off.

---

54 Craig Golden. "The Training of a Monkey Hunter," *American Falconer,* IX/4 (1997), pp. 7–10.

Hunting Eagles in the West

Friedrich Remmler was barely a figure of the nineteenth century, never mind the twentieth. He traveled in Central Asia just before a new empire walled it off again, filling its vast steppes with missile fields, nuclear test sites, and a spaceport. Born to rule, a self-described Teutonic knight by heritage, he never doubted his privileges. In his original memoir, *Reminisces,* published in English in 1970, he wrote: "I have persevered in the traditions all my life and have never veered from this path. Already as a young boy, I would have been a match for any Prussian nobleman or Baltic baron."[55] Reading him, the contemporary reader must wonder how anyone so arrogant could also declare himself so humble before nature.

In his native Finland, Remmler kept up to sixteen eagles at a time, plus a pack of hounds, a stable of horses, and a support staff of servants. He kept wolverines as house pets. His pronouncements were medieval: "Whoever has ridden hundreds of horses or has hunted with hounds will agree that no two animals are exactly alike, just as this is rarely the case with human beings. Only lame-brains and world do-gooders preach of the category, without believing a moment themselves, that all men are the same."

When he traveled to the steppes of Kazakhstan, he reveled in what he had found, often with humor: "The Kirghizian had many likeness [sic] to the modern Americans. They rode their horses even when the distance was scarcely 100 paces and the Americans today climb in their vehicles to go about the same distance."

He brought back Asian methods to his estates in Finland and later to Canada, where he ran a hunting plantation for General Motors, keeping until his last days his beloved wolverines and golden eagles. He probably had more experience than anyone else in the West with these birds, though his methods could be unorthodox by Asian

---

55 Friedrich Remmler. "Reminisces of My Life with Eagles," *The Journal of the North American Falconers' Association*, vol. XII and XIII (1973 and 1974), pp. 40–54.

standards (he didn't use a hood) and perhaps more fitted to those that might be employed by a medieval baron. Here he is describing the training of a favorite:

> I pictured this one as a wolf-eagle. After she had her basic training behind her, I began training her for the hunt and indeed only for wolves. A woman animal caretaker at my farm had a twelve-year-old son, who was very small, who played the wolf. A true artist in leather work . . . made him some armor out of strong leather. On the back of this was laid a wolf pelt with a large piece of meat tied to it. The first practice was in the area near the perch, since all hunting birds show more courage at home than in the field. As the boy loped [past] my eagle, she struck him immediately. I grabbed the bird quickly and set her on the perch and gave her the meat from the back of the boy.

It is easy to imagine such a character whipping his horse after quarry over the wheat fields of terrified peasants. But he had a deep appreciation for other cultures, at least ones that shared his love of the chase. He disdained both sides in the Cold War and contrasted them, both unfavorably, with a penniless Kirghiz nomad: "I asked the man if he would ever leave his homeland. The Kirghiz, who spoke Russian, got on his horse, made a sweeping gesture which Napoleon would have been able to envy, and said 'Leave this land: Has not Allah given us the steppe? Who is the measure of whether the gift of God is enough or not?' This man was a hunter by God's grace, and my teaching mentor." After being the first Western falconer to successfully catch wolves with a bird, Remmler gave up his beloved wolf hunting in a sudden fit of revulsion and later wrote, "The wolf should never be caught, poisoned, hunted with birds, shot or trapped."

Remmler left his perches and his legacy to a boy from a working-class town near Buffalo. Dan McCarron would later take them to the plains of the West, where he would refine them. Today he teaches biology to middle school students in a small Wyoming town, catching many foxes and even coyotes with perfectly mannered passage golden eagles: Remmler's legacy.

Another accomplished eagler in the United States is Charles Browning, whose tiercel (male) eagle was reverently named "Messiah." Browning previously specialized in hunting the turkey-size prairie birds known as sage grouse with gyrfalcons, but he had three killed by practical golden eagles. (This is not an uncommon occurrence anywhere falcons are flown and is why Arab falconers despise eagles, which is covered in the next chapter.) Eagles are also important sage grouse predators, capable of catching the birds in the air like a game falcon. Browning decided to fly an eagle. He has succeeded and no longer needs to fear the bigger birds.

Lauren McGough (right) and friends at Opocno pose with game.
Lauren McGough

In continental Europe a few eaglers inspired by Asians attempted to fly goldens before World War II, but eagle falconry didn't really take off until the 1970s. Today there are many accomplished eaglers in Germany, Austria, and Eastern Europe, specializing in hunting hare and roe deer. There is a large international meet each fall in Opocno in the Czech Republic, and many of both species are caught, with hares in the stubble and roe in rapeseed fields. Currently a video

Eagles await the flush in a rapeseed field near Opocno in the Czech Republic. Lauren McGough

showing an eagle dispatching a roe as easily as a goshawk catches a rabbit is making the rounds on the Internet, causing much disbelief among American hunters, who think it is staged or faked. In fact it is a common occurrence. As a friend, writer John Derbyshire, says, *"Aquila non capit muscas."* A young female eagler who was there in 2006 wrote to me:

> They have really mastered off-the-fist/out-of-the-hood flights with eagles. One that stands out in my mind: a male golden powered in after a brown hare, which leapt up several feet at the critical moment. The eagle rolled over, two great yellow feet shot out, and snagged it in mid-air! That's when you can't help but laugh and smile in the field!
>
> The photo . . . was a stunning field that was full of roe deer. The cover was about waist high. More than a dozen got up and running in the short time it took us to cover it. It's a bit intimidating to have something so large suddenly stir at our feet and gallop away! I couldn't believe they flushed just like rabbits. Several eagles connected, but didn't quite get a good hold . . . There's nothing quite like a roe galloping away and an eagle, seemingly slow-moving, just eating up the ground behind it. After several unsuccessful flights, a young doe got up and running. A first year female golden was released that tore through the air determinedly after it. She secured a head hold and the falconer sprinted to her side. I was that particular bird's first roe, which made for an especially good day.[56]

---

56 Lauren McGough. Personal communication.

Al Gates in his youth poses with his first eagle, Maria. ALAN GATES

In England there is also a tradition of hunting with eagles, though fewer have done it. Perhaps there is less suitable country, at least in the south, and a more sentimental attitude towards quarry. The first English eagler of note was William Humphrey, born in 1881 and best known as a breeder of English setters. He apparently kept few written records, but according to others he was a falconer of great abilities.[57] He reputedly used one of his setters to point foxes in the bracken while his eagle circled above and was said to have killed over one hundred.

Today England's most accomplished eagler may be Yorkshire's Al Gates, who has also traveled in Central Asia. He started at nineteen with an already trained, sweet-natured male and succeeded brilliantly,

---

57 Derry Argue. *Pointers and Setters* (Shrewsbury, 1983), p. 54.

HUNTING WITH THE KIRGHIZ

From _Unknown Mongolia: A Record of Travel and Exploration in North-West Mongolia and Dzungaria_, volume 2; Douglas Carruthers, 1914

The Kirghiz, and occasionally the Chantos, have a much more sporting way of hunting gazelle, by means of trained golden eagles, called in Turki "bouragut." This method is only attempted in winter, when the game is easy to approach, and the sportsmen have plenty of time on their hands. Often we saw a man riding along with a hooded eagle on his well-gauntleted right hand. The great weight of the bird is supported by means of a forked stick for the wrist, which fits into a socket in the front of the saddle. We were never fortunate enough to see a flight; but Major Cumberland, in _Sport on the Pamirs and Turkestan Steppes,_ gives such a good account of a kill he witnessed on the Tarim east of Aksu that I cannot do better than quote his description.

"I was anxious to see the eagle work, and, as I could see nothing of a stag, went off with the Yuzbeggie in the afternoon to try for another jeran. I was mooning along thinking of something

only to lose the bird to the unaffectionate embrace of a young female that was his intended mate.[58]

"Maria" took a long fourteen years to bond, but when she did she also became a great hunter. She bonded sexually with Al and built nests with him in the spring. He also trained a male semen donor from the

---

58 Alan Gates. Personal communication.

else, when all of a sudden the Yuzbeggie started off as hard as he could gallop across the maidan (plain). I followed suit, and soon made out a doe jeran in the distance. It stood and looked at us in amazement, and then cantered off, not very fast, while we still continued our headlong career, every now and then floundering on to our noses over a tussock of grass or into a hole hidden by the snow, until we got to about a hundred yards from our game, which only then realized the situation, and extended its stride. The shikari now hurled the eagle, which he had unhooded and held clasped to his breast during the run, at the jeran. The eagle, instead of rising like a falcon and sweeping on its prey, flapped along with its great wings quite close to the ground; and, although it seemed to fly very slowly, gradually caught up the jeran, which was impeded in its course by the high grass, and at last grabbed it by the rump with its strong talons. It regularly dragged the deer down, and held on for some time, the little gazelle kicking like mad. We still galloped on, and I wondered what the finish would be. The shikari, when he got up to them, without drawing rein threw himself off his pony, and grabbed the deer by the hind-leg, just as it had kicked itself free, and, pulling out his knife, cut its throat."

Royal Zoological Society of Scotland and artificially inseminated her. Ten years later he successfully reared a male, "G'kar." He writes to me:

> G'Kar grew with his mother and with my family of dogs and ferrets and cattle. This lack of fear of anything did pose some problems in later hunting.

An older Gates poses with Maria's son, G'kar. Alan Gates

> I had hoped that I could relax a bit, hunting a male
> eagle at rabbits, without the fear of a capable deer
> hunter over the now ever-crowded hills. G'Kar did
> not understand this, and took on any deer that
> ran and any fox as well. As luck would have it, I
> managed to curtail this enthusiasm through selective
> hunting ground, but it is still a worry.

Because of his exploits, Al was until recently the only Western
eagler recognized as a *"berkutchi"*—eagle hunter—by the Society
of Berkutchi in Mongolia. Now Lauren McGough, the young eagler
quoted earlier, has spent a Fulbright year there and become the first
female *berkutchi* ever, but she will write her own tale, I hope soon.

But those "ever-crowded hills" and a society ever less-
understanding of country matters are becoming a problem in the West.
In the 1990s a Sunday supplement article in one sensational British

tabloid condemned hunting with eagles in the most lurid of terms. "A Death Too Cruel" defined falconry as "the ruthless destruction of wildlife by birds of prey" and said that falconers "took delight in the pain and final tearing to pieces of kicking bodies." Eagles were "not the prettiest birds in the world" and "sky sloths," but Grizelda, the featured bird, nevertheless was somehow capable of "homing in on her unfortunate prey at speeds of up to 60 mph." After explaining how Grizelda had been "skillfully trained to savage on sight, spilling blood on the snow-covered landscapes and tearing flesh from the very bones of her victims," the writer finished: "When eagles, like Grizelda, get locked on their prey, they've been known to fly straight into fences of high-voltage wires. And, according to some of the locals who hate the thought of a killer eagle on their doorstep, the sooner Grizelda and her master finish up this way the better."

It seems that the myth of the Evil Eagle lives and that, as in the time of King James I, falconry is still "an extreme stirrer-up of passions."

CHAPTER 4

EAGLES AS ENEMIES

"They abhor eagles and vultures and all birds of prey that hover on high . . . "
—Patrick Leigh Fermor

The "Taung Baby" is one of the crown jewels of hominid paleontology, but it has always been a controversial fossil. The "baby"—more like a four-year-old child—is a specimen of *Australopithecus africanus*, a "hominin" precursor to *Homo sapiens*. Australopithecines were smaller and often more graceful that our kind, with an upright posture like ours but brains more akin to an ape's. The earliest australopithecines might have evolved five million years ago, and they were definitely present in their African home a million years later. The last ones may have survived until only 750,000 years ago.

The first *Australopithecus africanus* specimen, in the form of the Taung Baby, was dug from a South African limestone quarry in 1924 by Raymond Dart, a young professor of anatomy from the University of Witwatersrand. Dart spend four years chipping it from its limestone coffin. He immediately believed it to be a transitional creature between ape and man, but the conventional wisdom at that time did not agree. The so-called "Piltdown Man" skull from England, with its large cranium and apelike jaw, flattered scholars who believed our superior brains came first. Unfortunately for them it was a deliberate hoax compounded of a human skull, chimp teeth, and an orangutan's jaw, but it was not exposed until 1953.

Robert Ardrey's popular 1961 book, *African Genesis* (otherwise notorious for its "Killer Ape" hypothesis, reflected in the opening scenes of the movie *2001: A Space Odyssey* when the ape kills his companion with a bone), had the positive result of turning the world's attention to Africa as humankind's crèche. Ardrey, like Dart, believed that the young creature had been killed by a leopard or saber-toothed cat. But in 1995 anthropologists Lee Berger and Ronald Clarke wrote

Merry Christmas, from the Evil Bastard Killer Eagles

... they kill australopithecines

... and, worst of all, their own feathered brethren

... and little baby cows

And Merry Christmas 2004 from Darren Naish too

The myth of children carried off by eagles is backed in part by some scientific truth, thus paleontologist Darren Naish's 2004 Christmas card, all valid instances of eagle predation, is done with black humor.
DR. DARREN NAISH

a paper claiming the child had been killed by an eagle, as had other creatures in the fossil midden where it was found—small mammals, springhares, and antelope. There was no evidence of carnivorous mammals on the site, and marks like those made by an eagle's beak scarred the orbits of the skull's eyes. There were even bits of eggshell! (Paleontologist-taxonomist-blogger extraordinaire Darren Naish has produced a hilarious Christmas card commemorating the demise of the Taung Baby and other creatures mentioned in this chapter.) The probable culprit was once again that wild-eyed killer of primates, *Stephanoaetus coronatus*. Said Berger "The world was a cruel place for early hominids."[59]

Large eagles may eat their prey on the spot, but probably not in this case. Naish has written:

> . . . Anders Hedenström . . . showed in *Nature* that, given that *Stephanoaetus* can carry animals weighing just over six kilograms (wow!) then it would have to have dismembered the australopithecine. Which is fine, given that the specimen is only known from its skull. So, to those people who have suggested that the Taung eagle killed the australopithecine there on the spot (oh, I see, coincidentally in the middle of a veritable midden pile of eagle-killed small mammals), I say check out the literature on eagle lifting abilities.

The world may still be a cruel place for small primates, and *Stephanoaetus* may prey on primates larger than vervet monkeys. The artist David M. Henry, who both painted and trained crowned eagles, lived for a time in Zimbabwe and found part of the skull of a young human in a nest.[60] According to South African naturalist

---

59 Gore. "The First Steps," *National Geographic*, vol. II (1997), p. 96.
60 Steyn. *Birds of Prey of Southern Africa*, p. 111.

A child carried off by eagles is a persistent myth. THE LIVING WORLD,
ILLUSTRATED BY J. W. BUELL (PHILADELPHIA, PA, 1889)

The enormous Haast's eagle, which evolved to prey on moas, probably also attacked the early Maori settlers before they wiped out its food source. John Megahan/The University of Michigan Museum of Zoology

Peter Steyn: "That preying on young humans may very occasionally occur is borne out by a carefully authenticated incident in Zambia where an immature crowned eagle attacked a 20 kg, seven-year-old schoolboy as he went to school. It savagely clawed him on head, arms and chest, but he grabbed it by the neck and was saved by a peasant woman with a hoe, who killed it, after which both eagle and boy were taken to a nearby mission hospital. The boy was nowhere near a nest, so the attack can only have been an attempt at predation." (Nor are "immatures" territorial, though they may be more reckless than seasoned adults.)

Another possible human predator was the greatest eagle of all, New Zealand's recently extinct *Harpagornis moorei*. *Harpagornis* apparently evolved to prey on moas—enormous flightless birds that populated the two islands and occupied the niche that grazing mammals, which never reached New Zealand, hold elsewhere. Like humans, moas were erect and bipedal. In *The Lost World of the Moa*, biologists Trevor Worthy and Richard Holdaway speculate:

> Eagles not unexpectedly made an impression on the Polynesian settlers. Although it can never be known for certain, it is possible that eagles killed people, just as people killed eagles. The birds were certainly powerful enough to do so, and their claws were much larger than those of the Mongolian golden eagles that can—and do—kill the falconers who fly young birds against wolves. Accustomed as they were to feeding on large bipeds, the eagles could have mistaken the newcomers for a bizarre new form of the old quarry, a mistake that would have been all the easier if the human was wearing a sealskin cloak or one made of moa feathers. Whatever the reason, eagles seem to be among the birds depicted in rock paintings from the earliest period of Polynesian settlement. The most recent find, which is difficult to photograph satisfactorily because it appears only when the rock surface is damp from rain or mist, is reported to be an undoubted representation of an eagle, and a fine one.[61]

The eagle lasted until about AD 1350. A couple of hundred years after humans reached the islands, they had eaten all the moas and

---

61 Worthy and Holdaway. *Lost World of the Moa*, p. 223.

irrevocably altered the landscape by burning the native vegetation. Unlike moas, humans could fight back, and the world's largest eagle disappeared. However, there has been a recent reincarnation in popular culture. In the television show *Walking with Prehistoric Beasts*, a fine jungle eagle is shown preying on the ancestors of the Maori. It is portrayed as something like a harpy, boldly marked, with a crest and a long tail. While the build is correct, its ornaments seem more ornate that those of its near relatives in the genus *Hieraaetus*. But it is an improvement over the version in David Attenborough's (otherwise superb) *Life of Birds*, where the great eagle is "played" by an Arizona Harris's hawk!

Although, as has been said, eagles cannot lift the weight of a human child off the ground, mention should be made of the account in *The Living World* of a "well-authenticated" attack in the Alps, presumably by a golden eagle. "This event was said to have happened in 1838, and that though a rescuing party went promptly to the aid of the victim she was not recovered until life was rendered extinct from wounds received in her breast."[62]

Should an eagle slay and devour your hawk before your eyes and then clean its talons in the ground, and should you, having with you a Charkh trained to eagles, cast it at the eagle, and then execute various mutilating punishments on it—why, what delight can equal this?

Aeschylus

As stated in the first chapter, it is alleged that in the fifth century BC, Greek dramatist Aeschylus was killed when an eagle dropped a tortoise on his head. While not an instance of eagle-on-human predation, it is one of a human being used by a food-gathering eagle—and a good tale besides. According to the legend, Aeschylus was told that on a certain day (but uncertain year) he would be killed when a house fell on his head. A provident man, he made sure that he spent that day each year

---

62 H. S. Smith. *The Living World* (Philadelphia, 1889), p. 435.

REVENGE

From *Baz-nama-yi Nasiri: A Persian Treatise on Falconry*; translated by Lt. Col. D. C. Phillot, 1908

I once was flying a favourite passage-saker at a heron, and the falcon had rung up into mid-heaven and was on the point of taking the quarry, when suddenly an eagle appeared and seized my falcon in mid-air and slew her. I and my men galloped after the brute to rescue the falcon, but she was dead. The bastard that had made my liver into roast meat went and settled on a rock, but I had with me only a sparrow-hawk net, and with a sparrow-hawk net it is not possible to catch an eagle; for an eagle will not come to a sparrow-hawk net, or a sparrow-net—or if it does come, it carries it away. I suddenly spied a Kestril perched on a stone, and set up my sparrow-hawk du-gaza in front of it. The poor bird, through vain greed, fell into the snare and into my clutches. I pulled a few hairs out of my horse's tail and made four or five

out in the open. Of course he was outside when a golden eagle spied his bald pate and dropped the tortoise from a great height to crack it—the tortoise's "house"—open.

As Jeff Watson states in his monograph on the species, " . . . this little fable illustrates that the habit of eagles dropping tortoises onto rocks to crack open their shells was well known to the ancient Greeks. Only comparatively recently has this piece of natural history been 'rediscovered' by anthropologists in parts of southeast Europe and the Middle East."

strong nooses, and I skinned the sparrow. I tied the feathers into the Kestril's claws and concealed the nooses amongst the feathers. I then half-seeled the kestril's eyes and cast it into the air, but the murderous eagle was not attracted; it ignored the kestril. Suddenly a buzzard (sar) appeared, and, stooping at the feathers in the kestril's claws, got entangled in the nooses. Adding to the feathers, and strengthening the nooses, I half-seeled the buzzard's eyes and treated it as I had treated the kestril. The buzzard rose in the air; the eagle saw it, and rose after it to rob from it those tempting feathers; little it dreamt that the hunter would be hunted. It rose and made a glorious stoop; then, its fingers inside those nooses, it fell to the earth along with the buzzard. I murdered the murderer and rejoiced. So great was my exultation you might have almost fancied my falcon had not been slain. Now, you see you should always have with you complete apparatus for all kinds of sport and fowling, even to fishing tackle, for each sport has its own particular delight.

Eagles as Thieves

While eagle-on-human predation mostly fades back into prehistory and myth, the war of humans on eagles still rages on. As long as people have kept domestic stock, eagles have preyed on them, from the time of the earliest nomads in Asia and the Middle East down to modern-day Asia, Africa, Scotland, Texas, and the Mediterranean. With the striking exception of the Kazakhs and Kirghiz, most "stockmen" loathe eagles to the point of irrationality and well beyond any actual harm they do.

(A local cowboy took issue with my Mongolian stories because he refused to believe that an Asian "sheepherder" culture, as he put it, would tolerate eagles in any way. He only relented when I told him they used eagles to hunt wolves, which he hated even more.)

The shepherds of southern Greece, as recorded by Patrick Leigh Fermor in *Roumeli*, are utterly typical. "As of old, good and evil omens are discovered in the flight of birds. They abhor eagles and vultures and all birds of prey that hover on high; they are minions of the Devil in league with all evil spirits; then these harbingers of peril hover above a caravan they are spying out the destination. Abomination for these birds also springs from occasional raids when new-born kids are carried piteously bleating into the sky."[63]

And yet, as is so often the case, eagles are not just enemies of the shepherds; they have magical properties. Leigh Fermor describes the haunting melodies one friend plays on a bone flute, and says that it "... is made from the longest bone from an eagle's wing. We know that this bird is abominated ... After shooting the eagle and cleaning the wing-bone by burying it, he would have had to neutralize its wicked *mana* by leaving it under an altar for forty days of purification and exorcism before daring to drill the stop-holes and put it to his lips."

As long as herders had limited weaponry, their hatred of eagles could have little effect. Even firearms could only be used at limited ranges and on particular eagles, and traps needed tending and maintenance. But the nineteenth century brought effective poisons like strychnine, and after World War II sheep ranchers in the American Southwest gave so-called "predator control" a high-tech twist: They began to hunt eagles in their own realm—the air.

A *Life* magazine photographer documented this practice in 1951 when it was still socially acceptable. In one remarkable photo he leans in over the shoulder of a shooter with a pump shotgun as the light plane dives down at a helpless fleeing eagle, silhouetted against

---

63 Patrick Leigh Fermor. *Roumeli* (New York, 1966), p. 40.

This photograph was taken for Life *magazine from the window of a plane in Texas circa 1951, as the shooter swooped in for a kill.*

A. Y. Owen/Time & Life Images/Getty Images

badlands peppered with brush: the eagle as prey, the airplane as eagle.

Although the bald eagle, the nation's symbol, was already protected, such distinctions meant little in the minds of obsessed protectors of lambs and kids. Besides, until they achieve their mature white heads and tails in their fourth year, bald eagles are dark and superficially resemble goldens, especially the younger goldens with their white wing patches and tail bases. Such similarities eventually brought at least paper protection to the golden in 1962 under the Bald Eagle Act.

It was needed. According to one book published in 1966,[64] a single eagle "hunter" claimed a yearly kill (of both species) of twelve hundred; another claimed twelve thousand over a twenty-year period. But in fact the act did very little at first. For one thing, the bill allowed and still allows the governor of any state where flocks suffer eagle predation to apply to "control" them. For another, in Texas and other places, the act was virtually ignored. (In much of the western United States, grazing is mostly practiced on large tracts of federally owned public land that is leased to stockmen. In Texas, as in Europe, most land is privately owned and less subject to government scrutiny.)

But change comes eventually, even in Texas. In 1975 Alfred Zimmerman, the manager of a "game preserve" stocked with exotics like axis deer, aoudads, and Indian blackbuck antelope, watched a helicopter chase down an eagle. Conservation writer Donald Schueler relates the scene in his *Incident at Eagle Ranch:*

> A golden eagle, one of several that frequented the
> place during the winter months, swept out of the
> sky above the Zimmermans. Directly behind it, at a
> slightly higher elevation, the helicopter was in close
> pursuit. The bird knew it was in trouble and feinted
> first toward and then away from the cliff; but the plot

---

64 Johanna Johnson. *The Eagle in Fact and Fiction* (New York, 1966), p. 80.

was evidently familiar with such tactics, he steadily maneuvered the helicopter into a position from which its quarry would present an easy target. The eagle, as Cecil Zimmerman would later testify, never had a chance. Cecil's father furiously blinked the lights of the truck; he could see the gunner turning his head to look down at them. But it made no difference. Three shots followed in rapid succession. The eagle's wings collapsed against its sides, then stretched again as the bird fell towards the slope.[65]

After a long period of stonewalling, the disgruntled copter pilot, who had fallen out with his friends over money, turned state's evidence. Eventually and against all local expectations, a rancher, a ranch manager, and a predator control trapper employed by the government were indicted with violating the Bald Eagle Act and the Airborne Hunting Act, which generally forbids hunting with aircraft. The rancher and manager were also specifically charged with killing eagles with the aid of a helicopter and the rancher with perjuring himself before a grand jury. Although some of the testimony was ludicrous—one witness testified that he had given a dead eagle to "my Mexican" to burn because he suspected it was "rabid"—the times were a-changing. On December 9, 1977, a Texas jury found them guilty on all counts, despite the fact that at that time only federal law, not Texas law, protected golden eagles.

None of this should obscure the fact that eagles, especially wintering concentrations of goldens, can be a problem for some stock-growers. The always-fair Schueler saw eighty or ninety eagles in one day on one Texas sheep and goat ranch he visited. In such situations some predation is inevitable, and legally or illegally stock-growers will find a way to deal with it. A multimillion-dollar industry is at

---

65 Donald Schueler. *Incident at Eagle Ranch* (San Francisco, 1980), p. 3.

issue, and thousands of people depend on it for a livelihood, not to mention that it is the economic base for hundreds of small, isolated communities with no other industry.

One modern solution, now mostly illegal in the United States, was poisoning. Since the nineteenth century, strychnine, derived from the seeds of an Indian tree, was the tool of choice. It produced an agonizing death, not only for the target animal but also for anything that fed on the target's carcass and so on in turn. But strychnine had a strong odor, and mammals at least could learn to recognize the smell and avoid it. During the 1950s and 1960s it was largely replaced in the United States by sodium monofluroacetate, known as "Compound 1080," which was invented in World War II as a rodenticide. First used as such on the plains against prairie dogs, it soon began to decimate the whole food chain, for it was odor-free and toxic even at the third remove. It may well have driven the black-footed ferret, an obligate prairie dog predator and congener, to the brink of extinction, and its effect on other rare predators like the swift fox has not yet been calculated. It killed many hawks and more eagles, which are fonder of carrion. But although cattlemen and sheepherders made dire predictions about the effects of a ban, predation has not increased significantly, probably because the most significant predator, the coyote, makes up its losses by simply having more pups when it suffers higher mortality.

While slower in the West and other rural areas than in more urban parts of the States, the "paradigm shift" to a more benign view of predators has penetrated even there. Between 1987 and 1989 the Tigner family of ranchers in New Mexico's Socorro County (my home) reported to Animal Damage Control that they had lost six calves and had thirteen injured by a pair of golden eagles; allegedly a film exists of the birds attacking a calf. Rather than shooting the eagles, they cooperated in trapping and relocating them. Perhaps an anecdote might illustrate the changing scene: When I first moved here, a young rancher, knowing that I hunted with hawks, brought me a goshawk he had caught killing his prized and expensive game fowl. He had already tamed it. Though pleased, I was puzzled; why had he not shot it? "Hell," he said, "he's way neater'n any old chicken!"

Nowadays the preferred method of dealing with eagles is for the government to trap and relocate them. Curiously, this is also now the main source of eagles for American falconers; the two- to four-year-old birds that make up the bulk of this unsettled population are the ideal age for training. All of Dan McCarron's eagles started out as "depredating" birds. Soon, under new regulations, all American falconry eagles may come from this pool. Worries mentioned above—and held by many bureaucrats and even some falconers—paint the eagle started as an eyas, or nestling, as dangerous because it has lost its fear of humans, though Kazakhs would be skeptical.

There are still a few incidents of ranchers killing eagles here and there, but legal, organized, or aerial killing is a thing of the past, and the West is the better for it. Schueler wrote prophetically back in 1980 that "the predators are our test. Finally, the issue is not so much how we should manage them—as how we should manage ourselves."

Humans are a possessive species; they imagine that they own not only their genetically modified domestic livestock but also desirable wild animals. From the King's game to the grouse moors of Scotland and the partridge shoots of Spain, to ranchers managing white-tailed deer for trophy in Texas and even to the high-desert public lands of the interior western United States, predators have been accused of stealing "our" game. Eagles have gotten off relatively lightly on these grounds compared to smaller raptors; though the sea eagle was exterminated in Scotland, the golden hung on there and everywhere (and both were considered sheep-stealers rather than grouse poachers).

But the old tales can gain a new foothold in changing times. The West's land-use patterns are under siege in the twenty-first century. Vast public grazing lands still exist, but the riparian valleys that anchor them are falling, first to farming and then, even more destructively, to suburban development. The populations of even common species like mule deer suffer. Rarer species, like the bustard-size sage grouse, are on the edge of being declared endangered. Golden eagles obviously eat some sage grouse but are hardly the reason for their decline. And they are even less of a threat to hoofed animals. But here is a typical post from the *King's Outdoor World* blog:

> On the Salmon and Snake rivers in central Idaho we have been watching Golden eagles kill Mule deer and Bighorn sheep for years. They will actually grab a fawn or a lamb and fly a few feet with it and drop it. The country is steep and the fall starts it rolling down the mountain and injuries it so the eagle has easy pickings.
>
> We've also seen the eagles catch mule deer on the rock ledges and worry them to the point that they lose balance and roll off the mountain—again, easy pickings.
>
> These are the reasons that Golden eagles were shot on site until about the 1960s. We still think that there are too many eagles in this country.

I do not doubt that they have seen what they allege. I do doubt that all the eagle predation in the state of Idaho has the impact of ten "ranchette" developments.

Still, it may be the paradigm has well and truly shifted. A number of years back I heard a truck in my driveway and went out to find a party of elderly Navajos, one of whom was gently cradling an enormous female golden wrapped in a blanket. The young interpreter showed me the bird's broken toe and explained that they had caught it in a steel leghold trap set for coyotes. They wanted me to bring it to the raptor rehabilitation center—and they were sheepherders!

American photographer Edward Curtis, famous for his work with Native Americans, took this image of a Hidatsa eagle hunter.

Indians as Enemies

Native American reverence for eagles may ironically now be one of the greatest threats to the two North American species. Many Plains tribes traditionally trapped eagles by building pits, covering them with logs, and putting a bait on top. The trapper would wait below until an eagle landed on top and then reach up and grab its legs. Such trapping had little effect on populations; besides, the preferred birds for feathers were the nonbreeders under four years of age, with their dramatic black-tipped white tail feathers, and removing these has far less effect than targeting breeding adults or nestlings.

But recently environmental activist Ted Williams, a staffer at *Audubon* magazine, has written a scathing exposé on the Web titled "Golden Eagles for the Gods,"[66] which suggests that greed and the commoditization of eagle parts has resulted in making Indian consumers as great a threat to eagles as Texas ranchers once were.

The Pueblo tribes of New Mexico and Arizona have always taken nestlings in the spring and kept them on the flat adobe roofs of the pueblo, where they are honored, fed, and treated kindly until July, when they are smothered in cornmeal and sent as messengers to the gods. When eagles were more common, the Indians, like falconers, would always leave one in the nest. Now that the eagles are more rare, both nestlings are generally taken if there are two. Raptor biologist David Ellis says that he ". . . view[s] the Hopi [pueblo] reservation as an aquiline black hole." Another biologist, this one employed by the Department of the Interior, says: "We might as well be putting DDT out there. There are no young birds coming along. We have absolutely no way to justify handing out forty take permits."

Worse still is the commoditization of eagle feathers and parts. By law, all such things used in ceremonies or in the increasingly commercial powwow ceremonies must come from the federal Eagle Repository, a

---

66 Ted Williams. "Golden Eagles for the Gods," *Audubon* magazine web column: http://magazine.audubon.org/incite/inciteD103.html.

The prize for many Native societies was the coveted black and white tail feather of an immature golden. Bernardo Martino/Bigstock.com

"bank" of eagle parts compiled from the moulted feathers of captive eagles and from dead specimens. (Only Hopis are still allowed to take living eagles, and only Indians—and the infinitesimally small number of eagle falconers—may possess eagle feathers.) But the prices of feathers, talons, wings, and objects made from them are becoming so high that the incentives to ignore the law are enormous. A tail from an immature bird may bring four hundred dollars; a perfect "deck" feather from such a tail's center, three hundred dollars. A whole carcass might bring one thousand dollars, and prices are rising. According to Williams:

> Indians frequently argue that commercial powwows
> are part of their religion, but they're no more
> religious than rodeos. Some dancers make their
> livings going from powwow to powwow, competing
> for cash prizes. The Mohegan Wigwam Powwow
> at Uncasville, Connecticut, is typical, offering 'over

$50,000 in prizes for Dance Competition.' Powwow
contestants are judged, in part, by the feathers they
wear. During the 'grand entry' dance at the annual
Albuquerque powwow, you can see the remains of
at least twenty thousand eagles bouncing around the
floor at one time.

Such prices drive a cruel trade. Williams cites a member of the
Jemez tribe who claimed to have killed almost ninety eagles in 1995–
96. He told of catching six at once by setting traps around a cow
carcass. He graphically described how to dispatch an eagle by sitting
on it, getting it to bite a stick, and suffocating it. "They jump around
for ten or fifteen minutes." Another collector, a Navajo, said, "I'm like
most Navajos. If I see an eagle, and I've got a gun, I'll take a shot at it."

Even Hopis are tempted; in 1998 nine were arrested and convicted
of selling holy items made from feathers in violation of the (Indian-
supported) Native American Graves and Repatriation Act, mostly
directed at white collectors and museums. They served six-month
sentences.

Such abuses of tradition may be harder to stop than the aerial
predator control was because they are rooted in Native religion.
While not all Indians feel this way (in fact, probably a majority do
not), some activists are unbending. Williams confronted Susan Harjo
of the Indian rights group Morning Star Institute, and she accused
environmentalists, and by implication Williams, with racism:

"You find a lot of environmentalists who are only too happy to
appropriate the words of Chief Seattle [whose famous speech was
written, incidentally, not by the actual chief, but by a Hollywood
screenwriter], or take the thinking of other great people of native
history about the environment. Anti-Indian racism is rampant among
the environmental community." Williams persisted and asked her if all
Native Americans should be able to kill wildlife where they wanted,
even in National Parks: " . . . she replied with an emphatic 'Yes . . . if

you are exercising your religion it doesn't matter what other people think of it.'"

Such attitudes, backed by a sense of righteous anger and resentment, are even more resistant to change than those of other eagle-killer cultures. As Williams dourly observes, ". . . confronting Native Americans on wildlife exploitation is something the environmental community is terrified of, lest it be perceived as unsympathetic toward liberal causes such as racial and religious tolerance and the view of nature as that written for Chief Seattle." Probably reform must come from within, from Indians like members of the Hopi Eagle Clan, truest "owners" of the sacred birds, who sometimes sneak in and release rooftop eagles before they can be sacrificed. A member of that clan asked of a Fish and Wildlife agent, "How would you like to be chained in the sun for eighty days?" It is a slow process; in 2006 the Northern Arapaho petitioned a court in Jackson, Wyoming, for the right to shoot and use bald eagles at will.[67]

Falcon versus Eagle

The oddest instance of anti-eagle activity is the hunting of eagles with falcons. It occurs in Arab and other Islamic falconry cultures and spreads through much of eastern falconry outside of (always) the Kazakhs and Kirghiz. A good example, if romanticized, was the scene from Charles McCarry's novel *The Old Boys* quoted in the "Eagles as Allies" chapter. Part of the antipathy toward eagles is practical. As mentioned elsewhere, they are "pirates," kleptoparasites, and worse—a trained falcon sitting on a sage grouse in America or a houbara bustard in Pakistan makes a double meal for an enterprising eagle. In Arab cultures a trace of religious revulsion felt by observant Muslims (and Jews—see "Eagles of the Mind") for the sacred birds of their pagan ancestors may be added. What is certain is that there is an element of enmity, of a hatred for the quarry unusual in hunting.

---

67 "Judge Grills Man Accused of Illegal Eagle Shooting," *Billings Gazette* (23 March 2006).

The falcon does not always evade the eagle. VADIM GORBATOV

Ancient accounts of eagle hunting with falcons abound with remarks about hanging, beating, and abusing the quarry. Some contemporary Arab falconry festivals discourage images of eagles (though they are perfectly willing to buy and sell Islamically dubious ones of sakers and gyrfalcons!).

The *Baz-nama-yi Nasiri*, a Persian treatise on falconry written in 1868, is a fascinating compendium of useful training lore and medieval medicine. Its section on training a *charkh* (saker) to kill eagles illustrates a bit of this attitude for the reader:

> As soon as the eagle takes to running like a chicken,
> one horseman must detach himself and intercept it
> in front. Now when that son of a dog sees that it
> cannot fly, that its path is blocked in front, and that
> shouts and yells arise on all sides of it, it will have

no recollection of the *charkh* that has fastened on to its back; from rage and bewilderment it will drive its talons into the ground. Now, my pupil, on no account must you treat this son of a dog like other quarry. Do not in your excitement cast yourself upon it. On no Account! On no account do so— unless you seek your own destruction. As soon as the eagle has convulsively clutched the ground, you must dismount in all haste, and approaching it from behind firmly place your long boot on its back just between the shoulders, and so render if defenceless. Then cautiously advance your further hand from behind it and firmly grasp its legs, keeping one leg on the eagle the while. Then cut its throat, split open its breast, bring out the heart, and feed your hawk. You must know that the flesh of eagles is greasy and indigestible, so do not overfeed your hawk or she will fall ill.[68]

A son of a dog, running like a chicken, with greasy indigestible meat; boots and daggers—one might get the idea that Taymur Mirza didn't *like* eagles.

---

68 Lt. Col. D. C. Phillot (trans.). *Baz-nama-yi Nasiri* (London, 1968), p. 113.

CHAPTER 5

THE FUTURE OF EAGLES

"Animals are not brethren, they are not underlings;
they are other nations, caught with ourselves in the
act of life and time . . . "

—Henry Beston

While eagles have affected our species in various ways throughout our history, we probably would be the same or very similar species without eagles. Eagles did not make us. Nor did we "construct" eagles, despite the claims of literary theory. But we may well, at least in the short term, construct their future. We now have an enormous impact on many eagle species, sometimes by malicious intent, sometimes by accident while we pursue other ends, and sometimes even by benevolence, though even that can have complicated ends.

The malicious, deliberate persecution of eagles is in many eyes now the least-important factor in their survival. Sheepmen, Native American feather poachers, even the shooters of migrants described below, all face legal consequences and increasing social disapproval. The Philippine eagle was once a prized trophy; now the possession of a dead example of the national bird, as in the United States, is a disgrace.

Habitat degradation and destruction is a much larger problem, especially in the tropical forest ecosystems, which are disappearing at a frightening rate. The Philippine eagle, now down to a roughly estimated five hundred pairs spread over three islands (only one island has been censused in any detail), was once shot deliberately; now it has been "rebranded" as a patriotic symbol. New York environmentalist Robert F. Kennedy Jr., who worked as a Peace Corps volunteer in the Philippines in the 1970s, lobbied the Office of the President there to change its official name from the old "monkey-eating eagle" to the less-distasteful "Philippine." While it sounds a bit like a marketing initiative, it is only fair. The bird's diet mostly consists of civets and lemurs, and "civet-eating eagle" lacks a certain *je ne sais quoi*. The Philippine eagle now has its own foundation.

The harpy eagle of Central and South America, while it inhabits a much larger range, also suffers from habitat destruction. The well-known American Peregrine Fund, originally established to restore the DDT-damaged peregrine population of North America and now involved in worldwide bird of prey conservation efforts, decided in the 1990s to make the harpy the experimental subject to determine if it was possible to breed large, long-lived, slowly reproducing forest eagles for reintroduction. As they often did with smaller birds, they pulled eggs from the birds after a short incubation period and put them in incubators, leading the birds to lay more than they would naturally.

They have, to date, produced thirty-four chicks. However, since these eagles have a prolonged "adolescence," learning to hunt over almost two years (the parents only breed every other year), the process of reintroducing them is slow. Ten birds, all wearing radio-tracking equipment, are now roaming the Selva Maya forest in the borderlands of Belize, Guatemala, and Mexico. Researchers, tracking them from the tops of yet-unexplored Mayan pyramids, will monitor their eventual, hoped-for breeding success. Researchers also hope that publicity of the harpy will make it easier to preserve the forest—a

One of the largest eagles, the harpy is found from southern Mexico to northern Argentina. Habitat destruction has pushed it to the edge of extinction in much of its range. BARBARA BRAND/SHUTTERSTOCK

Bald eagles and humans both prefer waterfront property.
PETER LATOURETTE

living and specific symbol for something too close, vast, and abstract to be easily seen itself.

The bald eagle's return was much less hands-on and, because of its high tolerance for humans, much more visible. Bald eagles prefer to live on ledges and near water; much the same can be said of *Homo sapiens*. Before the advent of persistent pesticides, which intensify as they work their way to the top of the food chain, bald eagles could be seen in New York harbor and Seattle in winter and all over Florida. They vied with goldens, as we have seen, to dine on Texas sheep. They were so abundant in coastal Alaska that they were bountied as alleged salmon destroyers. (Their population never declined there, as there were no crops to speak of and therefore little DDT.) After World War II their disappearance from most of the United States was surpassed only by that of the peregrine falcon; they hung on mainly at the opposite poles of Alaska and Florida.

The bald eagles feeding on salmon are by Tony Angell, who sees them often at his coastal home near Seattle. Tony Angell

Because of their instant recognition factor, bald eagles surpassed even the peregrine as the "poster child" for the campaign against persistent pesticides. After the general use of DDT was banned in 1972, they rebounded, at first slowly then quickly as the remaining residue decomposed. There are now bald eagles in most states, though their populations remain unbalanced—25,000 in Alaska, 1,312 in Minnesota, but only a single pair each in Vermont, Rhode Island, and the District of Columbia. (Regarding the last, that any eagle can nest in a city shows a remarkable degree of human tolerance!) Almost ten thousand now nest in the lower forty-eight, and in June 2007 the bird was taken off the federal Endangered Species List.

Unintended Consequences

The effect of persistent pesticides was one level of unintended consequence, but some such situations have had more-benign results. When the controversial Glen Canyon Dam was built across the Colorado River in 1963, backing up the river into the silty basin known as Lake Powell, no bald eagles inhabited the Grand Canyon ecosystem. As the dam trapped suspended sediment, the water below became clear, causing the growth of a green algae of the genus *Cladophora*. *Cladophora* provided a habitat for insects, and insects provided food for trout. Eagles were drawn to winter at Lake Powell and discovered a new "run" of spawning trout at Nankoweap Creek below the dam. Now a huge congregation of adolescent eagles gathers at Nankoweap to feed on the trout. As mortality in all raptors is highest before breeding age, the population is increasing.

Some even say that increasing populations of bald eagles can be too much of good thing. In Homer, Alaska, a local resident created a tourist attraction by feeding the birds. For more than twenty years, and until her death in 2009, the "Eagle Lady," Jean Keene, spread as much as thirty tons of fish cannery waste on the rocky beaches. Her feeding resulted in congregations of as many as five hundred eagles, making the place a mecca for wildlife photographers. But as an Alaska.com article warned, "Less commonly photographed is the industrial cone of the Split at the photographers' backs, where hundreds of gorged eagles linger atop light poles, fuel tanks, and radio antennae in a Hitchcockian spectacle of nature gone mad!"

Bald eagles often congregate in the winter.
VISCERALIMAGE/SHUTTERSTOCK.COM

The problems were not merely aesthetic. Late-season feeding encouraged birds to congregate rather than disperse and breed. The concentration of predators put pressure on sea ducks, cranes, and geese. It was possible that weaker individuals survived to pass on less-than-desirable genes. Eagles regularly attacked small dogs. A local conservationist derided the garbage-eating birds as "dumpster divers." Given the various unintended consequences, Homer, Alaska, passed a law in 2009 prohibiting the feeding of predatory birds.

Of course unintended consequences result whenever the worlds of human invention and nature touch. Zimbabwe's Lake Kariba, an artificial impoundment on the Zambezi River, drowned a productive wilderness and never lived up to its promises. It *did* vastly increase the incidence of malaria and crocodile attacks with its thousands of square kilometers of weedy shallows. But those shallows, bristling with dead-tree perches, were a boon for the fish eagle, and the visitor

The abundant and vociferous African fish eagle, a close relative of our bald, is one of the most studied eagles on earth. LUDMILA YILMAZ/ SHUTTERSTOCK.COM

is rarely out of sight of one of these white-headed sentinels. Scotland lost its white-tailed eagle in 1916 from persecution by shepherds. A determined restoration effort has brought them back as a breeding species. But now a study funded by the Scottish National Trust of eagles on the Isle of Mull has established that on that island alone, the eagles kill more than thirty lambs a year!

Perhaps one of the oddest instances of unintended consequences is the de facto "wildlife refuge" in the DMZ—the 2.4-by-155-mile no man's land between North and South Korea, perhaps the deadliest place on earth for human beings. Its inhospitality to humans now

The white-tailed eagle of Eurasia is the bald's closest relative.
BIRDS OF PREY BY JOSEPH WOLF

Steller's eagles, almost extinct in Korea, congregate in the DMZ.
BIRDS OF PREY BY JOSEPH WOLF

means that it is a green belt between the starving North and the heavily industrialized South. It is home to fifty-two mammals and two hundred bird species, including two of the rarest crane species in the world,[69] red-crowned and white-naped, and the rare Steller's sea eagle.

We never know when the latest unintended consequence will emerge. The West's banning of DDT obscures the fact that it was intended to benefit humans, and that many in Africa still see the pesticide as a weapon against the scourge of malaria. The most recent chemical to cause catastrophic raptor declines was the animal pain reliever diclofenac. While its effects acted more on carrion-obligate vultures than on eagles, which only sometimes eat carcasses, it nearly wiped out the vulture population of the subcontinent before Peregrine Fund biologists discovered the culprit.

Persecution

There are still a few places where direct persecution (for reasons unrelated to livelihood) can put pressure on a species. Migration choke points—peninsulas jutting out into large bodies of water pointing toward winter quarters, narrow corridors between the ocean and the desert—can bring enormous amounts of birds together for short periods of time. In cultures that admire birds, such places become birders' hot spots. In cultures that value birds differently, they can become death traps. On the island of Malta, twelve thousand shotgunners greet the spring migrants every year—game birds, songbirds, and birds of prey. Most European nations protect the second, all protect the third, and even game birds are totally protected in spring. Maltese hunters are peculiarly obsessed; they chase down birds in motorboats, use cassette-taped calls, and bless their guns in church. Unlike most hunters, who hunt at least partially because game is delicious, they hunt mostly for stuffed specimens, throwing away examples that are not good enough. And their impact on birds of prey is enormous. In her book

---

69 Peter Matthiessen. *The Birds of Heaven* (New York, 2001), p. 193.

This engraving by Scottish artist William Miller after J.M.W. Turner, "The Dead Eagle – Oran," was published in 1838. Wikimedia

Fatal Flight, Natalie Fenech estimates that Maltese shooters kill up to ninety-six thousand birds of prey, including many eagles, a year.

Sometimes cultures that protect birds and those that destroy them live within shooting distance of each other. The marshes at the Mediterranean's edge in Lebanon and Israel and those of Eliat on the Red Sea have always been important stopping points in the migrations of birds between Africa's wintering grounds and Eurasia. As much as 75 percent of Eurasia's birds pass through here in spring, including booted, snake, imperial, and spotted eagles. Resort development in both countries has erased much of this habitat, and the chaotic political situation in Lebanon has done little to rein in the local practice of spring shooting. The only remaining sanctuary is Eliat, on the Red Sea in Israel; it is one of the best places in the world to watch migrating eagles and other birds of prey.

Laws for Eagles

Enacting laws against harming eagles is one obvious way to attempt to preserve them. But other laws affect eagles as well—laws about chemicals and land use, laws about development. There are also laws about the *use* of eagles. The United Kingdom views tame birds of prey as private property and makes no laws about who shall have one; eagles can be bought and sold like dogs and cats. In other countries the situation can be more complicated and ambiguous. In Mongolia an eagler's license is like a hunting license in the United States: You go in, pay a nominal fee, and get the license (though I must wonder if remote-country Kazakhs even bother; they continued to fly eagles during the time of the Soviet Union, when it was forbidden).

The United States makes things considerably more complicated. There is a basic federal falconry law, above which no state can be more lenient, and then fifty different state falconry laws. Falconers must pass through the stages of apprentice (with sponsor), general, and master falconer, with examinations at each step. The falconer's mews or hawk lodgings must be inspected. Each stage allows more, more-difficult, and rarer birds to be flown; eagles are restricted to masters, and special housing is required. Currently, if you are rich enough, you may still buy a captive-bred (golden) eagle (no individual can own a bald except in Canada). Actually there is an ongoing debate if one can "own" a raptor at all; in the United States all wildlife is property of the state, though the laws are in the process of revision, and captive-bred

This painting by Thomas Quinn is of an injured eagle in a rehab center.
Thomas Quinn

birds may become property. These revisions will probably restore the use of eagles in falconry to "depredating" birds because of the alleged dangerousness of birds raised from chick-hood.

However ludicrous certain regulations may appear to be, they are nothing compared to when humans begin applying their regulations to other species. The US Channel Islands are a group of small islands off the coast of California, formerly privately owned and now belonging to the National Park Service (NPS). They are home to feral pigs, introduced deer and elk, to rare endemic plants, as well as to a unique little fox *(Urocyan littoralis)*, which is endangered.

When the NPS took over the islands, they began to remove (i.e., kill) all the exotic animals. Animal rights groups protested for the pigs, while sportsmen's groups lamented the loss of the (probably less harmful) deer and elk, which had grown exceptionally large antlers.

Bald eagles had once existed on the islands but had disappeared when DDT thinned their eggshells so that no eaglets hatched. They were replaced by the fiercer goldens, which ate piglets. When the state had successfully eradicated the pigs, the eagles turned to the cat-size foxes. Researchers attached radio collars to the foxes, which proved the eagles guilty.

Conservationists first thought to kill the thirty-plus unendangered eagles. Other conservationists were outraged, as were falconers, who were limited to "depredating" inland eagles but were not allowed to come to the islands to trap.

Finally the Santa Cruz Predatory Research Group was allowed to trap thirty-one golden eagles on the islands and release them inland, with transmitters of course so they could be monitored against return to the islands (they haven't). Now plans are under way to reintroduce the fish-eating bald eagles to keep the goldens at bay. A tangled web indeed!

Future Eagles?

Eagles will continue to be eagles, splendid and for the most part indifferent to our ways. Some of us will always be obsessed with them, love them, hate them, make art or "friends" of them. They don't care; they ask nothing but to go on their splendid old dinosaurian way, over our heads, in or out of our minds. They need us less than we need them. If we leave them a space—they cannot live in cities, though balds may yet—they may well outlive our restless species, as they predate it. If we don't, we might find that many will vanish, leaving only the eagles of the mind that we have created in their image. We will be the poorer for it, but I confess I doubt it will even happen. I suspect it more likely that Aquila will pass like a shadow over the last human ruins, casting a benign predator's glance at them as she hunts on down the wind.

The late Kazakh falconer, Manai, serenades his eagle. STEPHEN BODIO

Biologist John Carlson traps and bands both bald and golden eagles for population studies in Montana. JOHN CARLSON (ALSO ON P. 191)

Will the eagle fly over our ruins? VADIM GORBATOV

AFTERWORD

By Sy Montgomery

When I was a child, my father wore eagles on his shoulders.

They were only stylized silver images, the Army insignia for colonel. But each time I saw them on his uniform—pretty much every day, except when he was on a mission—I believed in the eagles as totems. Eagles were my father's familiars: like him, brave, strong, and fiercely protective. Even though they sometimes scratched my skin when I threw my arms around my father's neck, I loved those eagles. I believed in their powers. I believed that eagles were watching over our country, as was my father, and that together they would keep us all safe.

As I grew older I learned this was not true. When I was in first grade, my father was promoted to brigadier general. His colonel's birds were replaced by the only things I knew of higher in the sky than eagles can soar: stars. It was about this time that I began to read the newspaper with my father and there learned to my horror that our planet was facing threats so widespread and insidious that not even the heavens could protect us. It was so awful it was even killing eagles.

The word "pollution" was new to the American vocabulary back then, and it was a word with a plethora of meanings: garbage, chemicals, human and animal waste. Even chemicals that people had thought useful became poisons when insecticides like DDT got into the food chain and began weakening the eggshells of nesting eagles. Pollution, poaching, deforestation, human overpopulation—these were all words as new to the adult readers of the *New York Times* in the 1960s as they were to me as a first grader. What made their horrors real to me was that these anthropogenic evils were pushing even our national symbol, the bald eagle—the bird that stood for all we wanted to be!—to the brink of extinction.

I remember my astonishment, and then my outrage, as a small child: How could we let that happen? Could anyone imagine a world without eagles? And who would want to live there?

Certainly not I. And certainly no one who has read this extraordinary book. Steve Bodio has reminded us here of how eagles enrich the human soul. With unmatched eloquence, drawing extensively from art, literature, and his own travels and experiences as a falconer, Steve has shown us what we stand to lose, worldwide, if we allow our greed—be it for profits or land or offspring—to eradicate the creatures that rule the very skies.

This is a crucial moment in human history for us to understand our relationship with these emblematic creatures, a wonderful time for this book to appear. For our relationship with eagles, as the author shows, is fraught with contradiction.

We both love and hate eagles. We love to be inspired—but we hate to be compared and found wanting.

Our human powers are puny compared with the fierce, alien wildness of eagles. Their glorious and terrible strangeness is twofold: The first is that they are predators. Human relationships with predators have always been complicated—even those that are mammals like us. People choose the great, shaggy carnivores as symbols of their armies and nations. In some cultures predators are worshipped. In Sundarbans, along the Bay of Bengal, for instance, where tigers eat an estimated three hundred people a year, people pray to a tiger deity, Daksin Roy.

And yet, with few exceptions, humans try their damndest to eradicate big predators wherever they are found. In my home state of New Hampshire, where sheep farmers punished predators for every lost lamb, wolves and cougars were driven to extinction before the turn of the twentieth century. Tigers are almost gone throughout their homelands in Asia, where we have completely erased three of their eight recent subspecies in the last hundred years and reduced the numbers of other subspecies to fewer than thirty individuals. In Africa cheetahs are nearly extinct, victims of farmers who blame them for killing their livestock, and African lion populations have dropped 90 percent in the past twenty years. (The figures are probably similar for the stealthier African leopards, but no one really knows.) Interestingly, farmers excuse the carnage by decrying their victims' moral character. To this day, some Western ranchers insist wolves are "bad" because they like to kill and eat the very same animals we want to kill and eat—and they're better at it. In other words, predators are like us but better than us, so we should eradicate them.

But eagles are not just predators but predatory birds, and that puts them in double jeopardy. Most people like their birds eating seeds at the feeders—or sitting in the soup pot or on the Thanksgiving table. The thought of birds strong enough to kill us seems to many people . . . well, too disturbing to contemplate.

But not to Steve. A master of literature who is also trained as a biologist (a rare combination), he has known eagles as individuals (as varied in personality as we are) as well as symbols. He sees eagles for what they are. And they are, to our astonishment, powerful winged predators—direct descendants of the smart, fast, meat-eating therapod dinosaurs like *Tyrannosaurus rex* and velociraptor.

Eagles' ferocity comes as no surprise to the author of this book. After all, when he first tried to train an eagle in 1971, she broke his hand; when he visited Mongolia to hunt with falconers there, he learned of a golden eagle that attacked a snow leopard and another that killed a falconer's grandson. None of this made him afraid of eagles—Steve is as fearless a falconer as he is a writer. And none of this diminished his love for them.

This is one of the many blessings of this splendid book. It's true of all of Steve's writing: while most nature writers seem to yearn for the animals, plants, even the landscapes we love to love us back. Wild eagles will never do this. They don't need our affection. They don't need our admiration. Steve's is the only kind of love eagles need from us: the kind of love that lets eagles be wild and asks for nothing back. Look into the eye of an eagle. That should be enough.

Eagles inspire us with their courage and awe us with their grace. But perhaps most important to the survival of the human soul, eagles teach us reverence—a virtue that, writes classicist and philosopher Paul Woodruff, "begins in a deep understanding of human limitations." No other creatures show us our limitations better than do the birds. Steve Bodio shows that no other birds show us our limitations better than do eagles.

Our kind has surely accomplished brilliant feats during our short time on this earth as a species. But before we poison, pollute, degrade, and murder every other creature on the planet, we must learn to limit our numbers and our greed. This is the lesson that humans so desperately need to learn at this turning point in human history. We could have no better teachers than the eagles.

—Sy Montgomery

Sy Montgomery is the author of seventeen books on nature, including *Birdology: Adventures with Hip Hop Parrots, Cantankerous Cassowaries, Crabby Crows, Peripatetic Pigeons, Hens, Hawks and Hummingbirds.* She is also an ardent conservationist and a student of falconry.

INDEX

Evans, George and Kay, 100–101

Fabre, Jean-Henri, 122
Falcon (Macdonald), 107–8
falconry
    *Baz-nama-yi Nasiri: A Persian
        Treatise on Falconry,* 158–59
    in Central Asia, 122–35
    defined as, 107–8
    eagle hunting with falcons, 171–73
    and eagles as allies, 67, 107–49
    earliest evidence of, 64
    falconry laws in the United States,
       187–88
    hunting eagles in England, 145
    hunting eagles in the West, 140–49
    hunting with the Kirghiz, 146
    Japanese falconry, 135–37
    Kazakh and Kirghiz falconers,
       67, 107
    practice of, 84
    unusual eagle falconry, 135–39
Fenech, Natalie, 186
Fermor, Patrick, 160
Field Guide to the Birds (Peterson), 94
fish hawk *(Pandion haliaeetus),* 45–46,
    51, 53
Flannery, Tim, 21
Fleming, Peter, 117
Fowler, Jim, 106
Franklin, Benjamin, 78
Frederic II, Emperor of Rome, 85
Frison, George, 50
Fuertes, Louis Agassiz, 23, 38, 87

Gates, Al, 145–48
Gibraltar, 61
Glen Canyon Dam, 180
Golden, Craig, 138–39
golden eagle *(Aquila chrysaetos)*
    care and feeding of eaglets, 59
    characteristics of, 38–39

hunting strategies and prey, 37,
    48–51, 189
illustrations, 8, 38, 89, 93
mating rituals and nesting, 54, 55
migration, 60, 61
overview, 9–15, 13, 14, 37–41
shot on site until the 1960's, 166
weight, 38
Gorbatov, Vadim, 8, 95, 109, 114,
    119, 138
Grant, Gen. Ulysses S., 81
Great Seal of the United States, 81
Gruenwald, Andre, 138–39
Guatemala, 176

Haast's eagle, 155
habitat degradation and destruction,
    176, 177, 187
Handbook of North American Birds
    (Stalmaster), 46
Harjo, Susan, 170–71
Harpagornis moorei, 35, 156–57
harpy eagle, 7, 21, 46–47, 176–78
Harpy (movie), 103–6
Harris's hawk, 133
hawk eagle, 19, 35, 36, 136
Hawk Mountain, 60
Hawk Watch (Evans and Evans),
    100, 101
Hawking of Japan (Jameson),
    135–36
Henry, David M., 153
Hieraaetus eagle, 41
High Tartary (Lattimore), 115–17
Himalayan passes, 61
Hokkaido Island, 135
Holdaway, Richard, 156
Homer, AK, 61
Hopi Eagles Clan, 171
howler monkey, 46
Hughes, Ted, 15
Humphrey, William, 145